KU-613-374

Hamlyn's Guide
to Sauces
and Saucemaking

Hamlyn's Guide to Sauces and Saucemaking

Sonia Allison

Illustrated by Rosemary Aldridge

HAMLYN

LONDON·NEW YORK·SYDNEY
TORONTO

© copyright The Hamlyn Publishing Group Limited 1970
Published by The Hamlyn Publishing Group Limited
LONDON · NEW YORK · SYDNEY · TORONTO
Hamlyn House, Feltham, Middlesex, England
Printed in Czechoslovakia by Tisk, Brno

ISBN 0 600 02866 6

CONTENTS

6 Introduction

8 Simple White Savoury Sauces

18 Classic White Sauces

32 Classic Brown Sauces

46 Egg-based Sauces

76 Butter Sauces

82 Beurres Composés

91 Barbecue Sauces

95 Classic Italian Sauces

106 Miscellaneous Savoury Sauces

141 Quick Sauces

146 Salad Dressings

158 Sweet Sauces

181 Postscript

190 Index

Introduction

The Oxford dictionary defines sauce as a 'liquid preparation taken as relish with some article of food.' Which, considering the aristocratic sauces created in the 18th and 19th centuries, by such master chefs as Antonin Carême and Auguste Escoffier, is really a remarkable piece of understatement! Sauces were originally intended to enhance the foods with which they were served — and still are. They were not made to cover inferior cooking or to camouflage poor quality ingredients. They were, instead, regarded by their creators simply as important accessories which had to be gracious, elegant and subtle; never overwhelming or ostentatious.

Over the years a considerable amount of mystique has built up round sauces and many good cooks are prepared to by-pass the art completely, firmly believing that saucemaking should be left exclusively to the expert. Sadly, therefore, we return to what we already know, but don't necessarily love — watery gravy, bottled ketchup, an assortment of relishes and pickles and very plain white sauce enlivened, occasionally, with scraps of chopped, dried parsley or stale cheese.

The most interesting thing about sauces is the fact that they are much less complicated to prepare than most people imagine.

Almost every known sauce is a variation of a basic recipe and the great classics stem either from Béchamel, Velouté or Suprême (the white group), from Espagnole or Spanish (the brown group) or from Hollandaise and Mayonnaise (the egg group). Even salad dressings and savoury butters have basic recipes so that the whole process of saucemaking is simplified once the elementary rules and principles have been understood.

In France and Italy and many other European countries, no one thinks twice about making sauces; they do it as a matter of course because that's the way they've been brought up. Not with the same skill as Carême or Escoffier perhaps, but certainly with the same love and the same pleasure, knowing that a good, well-flavoured and smooth sauce, however simple, will add a gourmet touch to the plainest of meals and turn it into something which will be well appreciated and long remembered.

Throughout this book you will find recipes for every type of sauce, from the very simplest cornflour sauces to the famous families of classics. There are recipes for the traditional favourites to include bread, mint and apple sauces, among others, and for enthusiasts of Italian food, I have given a few recipes for their best known sauces, such at Bolognese and Neapolitan.

There are sections on Salad Dressings, Savoury Butters and Sweet Sauces and for those who need a tasty sauce in a hurry, I have included recipes for quick sauces made with canned soups. There are sauces for every occasion, for every meal, for every mood, and it is hoped that with this book in hand you will make delectable sauces for evermore.

Simple White Savoury Sauces

The simplest of all the white sauces are those made by blending cornflour or flour smoothly with milk, then adding a knob of butter or margarine (for gloss) and salt and pepper to taste. These sauces are inclined to be bland and are therefore suitable for children's dishes and invalid meals. Two thicknesses can be made; a pouring sauce for moistening foods and a coating sauce for covering foods. The sauces may be served with fish, poultry, offal, white meat, vegetables and egg dishes. Because the colour of these sauces is insipid (if they are served completely plain without additions) and because both children and invalids need food which looks appetising, an egg yolk, which will add extra nourishment as well, or a few drops of yellow or red food colouring may be beaten into the cooked sauces just before serving.

Any milk may be used, including canned evaporated milk diluted as directed, or skimmed milk made from instant non-fat milk granules. Sauces made with skimmed milk are especially recommended for those on light diets.

Reheating sauces: if the sauces are made in advance to be reheated and served later, they should be covered, while still hot, with a piece of damp greaseproof paper (when the paper is removed the skin will lift off with it) and cooled as quickly as possible to prevent thinning. If covered and held hot, steam will cause the sauces to thin down so that the entire consistency will be altered. To prevent sticking, burning and overcooking, the sauces should be reheated either in the top of a double saucepan or in a basin standing over a saucepan of gently boiling water.

1 POURING SAUCE

Cooking time 9—10 minutes *Serves* 4

½ oz. (1 level tablespoon) flour or cornflour
½ pint cold milk

small knob or 1 teaspoon butter or margarine
salt and pepper to taste

Blend flour or cornflour to a smooth cream with 2—3 tablespoons cold milk. Pour rest of milk into a saucepan and bring just up to the boil. Pour on to flour or cornflour cream, stirring briskly all the time. Return to saucepan. Cook over low heat until sauce comes to boil and thickens, stirring or whisking continuously with a wooden spoon, light balloon whisk or other hand whisk to prevent lumps from forming. Add butter and simmer very gently for 3 minutes so that the starch grains in the flour or cornflour are thoroughly cooked. Season to taste and serve hot.

2 COATING SAUCE

Make in exactly the same way as Pouring Sauce (see Recipe 1), but increase the flour or cornflour to 1 oz.

THE ROUX METHOD

The roux method comes a bit higher up the scale of white sauces which are made with a roux base of fat and flour. They need a little more attention than those made by the blending method but they have a superior flavour and are well worth the extra effort. A roux, which actually thickens the sauce, is made by heating together equal amounts of fat and flour. Butter is best for flavour, although good quality margarine makes a fair substitute, the flour can be either self-raising or plain. Because the quality, flavour and consistency of the sauce depends largely on the roux, a certain amount of care is necessary during its preparation. A heavy-based saucepan is the most suitable choice. Melt in it the butter or margarine until foamy. Keep the pan over a low heat and stir in the flour with a wooden spoon. Cook it slowly (the slowness is important because a roux for a white sauce must not be allowed to colour) for about 3 minutes, stirring all the time to ensure even distribution of heat and to prevent browning. Without this the starch grains will swell unevenly and will later be unable to absorb the liquid properly. Thus the sauce will be thin. This is the most important process and cannot be hurried because if the heat is increased the flour will scorch and the sauce will be bitter and thin.

Another very important factor, where smoothness of the sauce is concerned, is the temperature of the liquid and the way in which it is added. If the roux is freshly made and still hot, then the liquid should be cold or lukewarm. If the roux has been prepared ahead of time and is therefore cold in the saucepan, then the liquid must be hot but not necessarily boiling. *All* the liquid may be added to the roux at once but it is essential to whisk the sauce continuously with a hand whisk as it comes to the boil and thickens, otherwise lumps may form and the sauce will have to be strained.

For those unused to saucemaking, it is probably safer, although slower, to remove the saucepan containing the roux from the heat and then to add the liquid gradually, stirring well with a wooden spoon after each addition, until the sauce is very smooth.

Again the sauces can be made in two thicknesses, pouring and coating, and in their plain unadorned state may be served with fish, poultry, offal, white meat, vegetable and egg dishes.

If made ahead of time, see instructions for covering and reheating sauces on page 9.

3 POURING SAUCE — ROUX METHOD

Cooking time 9—10 minutes *Serves* 4

½ oz. butter or margarine
½ oz. flour

½ pint cold or tepid milk
salt and pepper to taste

Melt butter or margarine in a heavy-based saucepan. When foamy, stir in flour. Cook slowly for 3 minutes, stirring all the time. Remove from heat. Gradually add milk, stirring well after each addition (or add all the liquid at once). When sauce is smooth, return to heat. Cook, stirring with a wooden spoon all the time (or whisking with a hand whisk, depending on the method you've chosen), until sauce comes to the boil and thickens. Simmer over a low heat for 3—4 minutes, stirring frequently. Season to taste with salt and pepper and serve hot.

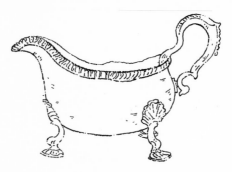

4 COATING SAUCE — ROUX METHOD

Make in exactly the same way as Pouring Sauce (see Recipe 3), but increase the butter or margarine and flour to 1 oz. each. The cooking time remains the same.

Variations: A flavoured sauce is more appetising than a plain one provided it harmonises with the food with which it is to be served. Thus a sauce for chicken should be made with approximately half milk ($\frac{1}{4}$ pint) and half chicken stock ($\frac{1}{4}$ pint); a sauce for fish with half milk and half fish stock; a sauce for mutton or lamb with half milk and half mutton or lamb stock; a cheese sauce for cauliflower with half milk and half cauliflower water; a sauce for bacon with half milk and half bacon stock — and so on. If home-made stock is not available, use chicken stock cubes and water for poultry and white meat dishes, and beef stock cubes and water for red meat, bacon, liver, tongue and heart dishes. A reasonably flavoured fish stock can be made by poaching gently for 30 minutes some fish heads and bones with water to cover, a peeled onion, 1 bay leaf, 1 or 2 cloves, a squeeze of lemon juice or 1 tablespoon white wine, a few parsley sprigs and salt and pepper to taste.

Pouring or Coating sauces, made either by the blending or roux methods, can be used as the bases of the following variations: —

5 ANCHOVY SAUCE

A mild fish-flavoured sauce, traditionally served with fried, poached, steamed, grilled or baked white fish dishes. It is, however, very good over eggs and with creamed or fried veal. Make up $\frac{1}{2}$ pint of Pouring or Coating sauce (see Recipes 1—4), and stir in 1 or 2 teaspoons anchovy essence and 1 teaspoon lemon juice. Season to taste. Reheat gently before serving. If the sauce is too pale, tint pale pink with a little red food colouring.

6 CAPER SAUCE

A piquant sauce which goes well with mutton, skate and the oily fish such as herrings and mackerel.
Make up $\frac{1}{2}$ pint Pouring or Coating sauce (see Recipes 1—4), using half milk and half mutton stock for mutton or half milk and half fish stock for the herring or mackerel dishes. Stir in 1—2 level tablespoons chopped capers and 1—2 teaspoons vinegar from jar of capers. Season to taste. Reheat gently before serving.

7 CHEESE SAUCE

A popular sauce which teams extremely well with vegetables, fish, poultry, ham, bacon and eggs. The type of cheese used is a matter of taste but the milder it is, the milder the sauce will be. Lancashire cheese makes a pleasant change from Cheddar, and any of the blue vein cheeses add a distinctive, if not traditional, flavour. If using Parmesan cheese, reduce the amount of cheese in the recipe by half.

For ease, make up ½ pint Pouring or Coating sauce (see Recipes 1—4), using all milk or three-quarters milk and either quarter vegetable water, fish stock, chicken stock, or beef stock, depending on the dish. Remove pan of sauce from heat and stir in 2—4 oz. finely grated or crumbled cheese, ½ level teaspoon made mustard and pinch of cayenne pepper. Stir until cheese melts but do not reheat or sauce may become stringy. Season to taste and serve immediately.

8 EGG SAUCE

An attractive sauce for poached, steamed or grilled white fish dishes and for poultry.

Make up ½ pint Pouring or Coating sauce (see Recipes

1—4), using all milk or three-quarters milk and either quarter fish or chicken stock, depending on the dish. Stir in 1 or 2 chopped (or grated) hard-boiled eggs. Season to taste. Reheat gently before serving.

9 LEMON SAUCE

A light and refreshing sauce, especially good with baked, poached, steamed or grilled white fish dishes and with roast poultry and veal.

Make up $\frac{1}{2}$ pint Pouring or Coating sauce (see Recipes 1—4), using half milk and either half fish or chicken stock. Stir in 1 level teaspoon finely grated lemon peel and 2 dessertspoons lemon juice. Season to taste. Reheat gently and serve hot.

10 MAÎTRE D'HÔTEL SAUCE

A creamy, elegant sauce usually served with steamed, poached, baked, grilled or fried white fish dishes. Make up $\frac{1}{2}$ pint Pouring or Coating sauce (see Recipes 1—4), using half milk and half fish stock. Stir in juice of $\frac{1}{2}$ small lemon, 2 level tablespoons very finely chopped parsley and 2 tablespoons fresh single or double cream. Season to taste. Reheat gently before serving, but do not allow to boil.

11 MUSHROOM SAUCE

Another popular sauce that goes with practically everything. Make up $\frac{1}{2}$ pint Pouring or Coating sauce (see Recipes 1—4), using all milk. Just before serving, stir in 2—3 oz. sliced mushrooms, freshly fried in about $\frac{1}{2}$ oz. butter or margarine.

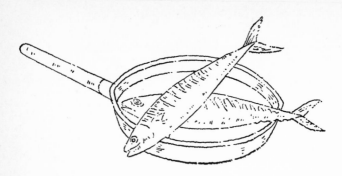

12 MUSTARD SAUCE

One of the best sauces to serve with ham, bacon and cheese dishes. It is also good with fried or grilled herrings and mackerel or hot tongue. English mustard is the usual one to use.

Make up $\frac{1}{2}$ pint Pouring or Coating sauce (see Recipes 1—4), using all milk or half milk and either half ham or bacon stock or half fish stock, depending on the dish. Stir in 1 or 2 level teaspoons dry mustard mixed to a smooth cream with 3 teaspoons vinegar. Season to taste. Reheat gently and serve hot.

13 ONION SAUCE

The perfect sauce for tripe, it is also delicious with roast lamb, grilled lamb chops, fried lamb cutlets, boiled mutton and boiled bacon.

Cook 2 medium skinned and chopped onions in boiling salted water for 10—15 minutes or until tender. Make $\frac{1}{2}$ pint Pouring or Coating sauce (see Recipes 1—4), using half milk and half onion water. Add all the onions (well-drained) and $\frac{1}{4}$ level teaspoon ground nutmeg. Season to taste. Reheat gently and serve hot.

14 PARSLEY SAUCE

A sauce well known by everybody. It needs plenty of fresh green parsley and a touch of ground nutmeg to give it flavour. It is good with boiled bacon, ham dishes, poached, steamed, baked or grilled white fish dishes and boiled mutton.

Make up $\frac{1}{2}$ pint Pouring or Coating sauce (see Recipes 1—4), using all milk or half milk and either half bacon, ham, fish or mutton stock, depending on the dish. Stir in 3—4 level tablespoons finely chopped parsley and a large pinch of ground nutmeg (or more according to taste). Season to taste and serve.

15 PRAWN OR SHRIMP SAUCE

A delicate and pretty sauce, suitable for poached, steamed, baked or grilled white fish dishes.

Make up $\frac{1}{2}$ pint Pouring or Coating sauce (see recipes 1—4), using all milk or half milk and half fish stock. Stir in 1—3 oz. chopped peeled prawns or shrimps, a squeeze of lemon and $\frac{1}{2}$—1 level teaspoon anchovy essence. Season to taste. Reheat gently before serving, but do not allow to boil.

Classic White Sauces

Learn young and you will learn fair

The Béchamel sauce is the first classic sauce or 'mother' sauce as it is known in France. Béchamel is named after Louis de Béchameil, Marquis of Nointel, who is believed to have created the sauce while he was *maître d'hôtel* at the Court of Louis XIV. It is, in fact, an extension of the simple white sauce made by the roux method except that the milk, instead of being plain, is first warmed with a number of additions which add flavour and a subtle, mild piquancy. Many variations stem from this celebrated classic and all have one thing in common — they are characteristically creamy with a fine, smooth flavour.

Butter should be used for the sauce; there is no substitute since no other fat ever produces quite the same high-quality flavour. As Béchamel sauce is usually used for coating foods, the proportion of butter and flour to milk is rarely less than 1 oz. to ½ pint.

Like the other white sauces, basic Béchamel may be prepared ahead of time and reheated, although variations containing eggs should be freshly made as reheating could cause separation and a curdled appearance. For covering and reheating instructions, see page 9.

For those with domestic deep freezers, here is a practical idea from America. Make up more basic Béchamel sauce than you actually need. Freeze it in an ice cube tray fitted with the usual dividers. Store in the deep freeze and then all you have to do is take out as many sauce cubes as you need and melt them down in the top of a double saucepan or in a basin standing over a saucepan of gently simmering water. Variations can then be made simply by stirring in appropriate additions when the sauce is hot.

Béchamel sauce can be served with steamed, poached, baked or grilled white fish and with poultry, egg and vegetable dishes. It is also the most usual sauce to use for filling vol-au-vent cases.

16 BÉCHAMEL SAUCE

Cooking time 13—14 minutes *Serves* 4
    plus standing time
    45 minutes

½ pint milk	2 cloves
1 small onion, peeled	4 white peppercorns
1 small carrot, peeled	1 oz. butter (unsalted for
½ small celery stalk	preference)
1 blade of mace	1 oz. flour
1 sprig parsley	salt and pepper to taste

Pour milk into a heavy-based saucepan. Cut onion into quarters. Slice carrot thickly. Break celery into 2 or 3 pieces. Add vegetables to milk with mace, parsley, cloves and peppercorns. Bring slowly to the boil, stirring all the time. Immediately remove pan from heat and cover. Leave to stand for approximately 45 minutes. Strain. Melt butter in a clean saucepan. When foamy, stir in flour. Cook slowly for 3 minutes, stirring all the time. (Do not allow roux to brown.) Remove from heat. Gradually add flavoured milk, stirring well after each addition (or add all the liquid in one go). When sauce is smooth, return to medium heat. Cook, stirring with a wooden spoon all the time (or whisking with a hand whisk if liquid has been added all at once) until sauce comes to the boil and thickens. Simmer over a low heat for 3—4 minutes, stirring frequently. Season to taste with salt and pepper and serve hot.

Variations:

17 CHAUD-FROID SAUCE

This literally means hot-cold sauce; hot Béchamel sauce (see Recipe 16) mixed with cold savoury jelly, such as aspic. When the sauce has cooled and thickened sufficiently to coat the back of a spoon, it is then used to coat cold buffet-type foods, such as halved hard-boiled eggs, portions of cooked fish, whole salmon and salmon trout (cooked, skinned and boned), portions of chicken, whole birds and ham joints. When the sauce has set completely, the dishes are decorated according to taste and coated evenly with a final layer of clear aspic jelly, which holds the decorations firmly in place. Make up $\frac{1}{2}$ pint Béchamel sauce. Stir in 3 level tea-spoons gelatine dissolved in $\frac{1}{4}$ pint boiling chicken, beef or fish stock, depending on the dish. Season to taste. Leave to cool until sauce has thickened sufficiently to coat the back of a spoon. Use straight away. Instead of gelatine and stock, $\frac{1}{4}$ pint aspic jelly (made up with a little more powder than usual) can be used.

18 DORIA OR CUCUMBER SAUCE

Named after an Admiral from Italy. It is a fresh looking sauce, delicious with poached, grilled, baked or
steamed white fish dishes, poached or grilled fresh
salmon, salmon or tuna fish cakes. If the sauce is too
pale, a few drops of green food colouring should be
stirred in just before serving.

Peel half a medium cucumber. Cut into fairly thick
slices and simmer in boiling salted water until tender.
Drain thoroughly and chop finely. Make up $\frac{1}{2}$ pint
Béchamel sauce (see Recipe 16), with all milk or
three-quarters milk and one-quarter cucumber water.
Stir in chopped cucumber, a large pinch of sugar,
$\frac{1}{4}$ level teaspoon ground nutmeg and 3 tablespoons
fresh double cream. Reheat gently without boiling.
Season to taste. Serve hot.

19 HORSERADISH SAUCE (hot)

A distinctive flavoured sauce which partners well with
beef roasts and grills, hamburgers, baked, fried or
grilled mackerel, herrings and trout.

Make up $\frac{1}{2}$ pint Béchamel sauce (see Recipe 16), with
all milk. Mix 2—3 level dessertspoons grated horseradish with 1 level teaspoon castor sugar and 1 teaspoon vinegar. Add to sauce with 2—3 tablespoons of
cream. Season. Reheat gently without boiling.

21

20 MORNAY SAUCE

Possibly the best known variation of Béchamel, and a sauce from which many other dishes get their names. For instance, poached sole with Mornay Sauce is known as Sole Mornay; hard-boiled eggs with Mornay Sauce are known as Eggs Mornay; hot crab with Mornay Sauce is known as Crab Mornay and so on. It is a superbly creamy and full-flavoured cheese sauce and adds an elegant touch to any food with which it is served. Gruyère or Parmesan cheeses are traditionally used although strong English or Canadian Cheddar are very acceptable substitutes and, in addition, give the sauce a rich, golden appearance.

Make up ½ pint Béchamel sauce (see Recipe 16) with all milk. Stir in 2 oz. very finely grated Gruyère or Parmesan cheese, or 3—4 oz. finely grated Cheddar cheese and a pinch of cayenne pepper. Stir or whisk gently until cheese melts but do not allow to boil or sauce may become stringy. Season to taste and serve hot.

21 MOCK HOLLANDAISE SAUCE

Sometimes known as Dutch sauce, this is a less rich sauce than true Hollandaise, but is nevertheless very good with poached, grilled or steamed fish dishes, with vegetables such as cauliflower and broccoli and with poultry.

Make up ½ pint Béchamel sauce (see Recipe 16) with approximately three-quarters milk and quarter fish stock, vegetable water or poultry stock. Stir in 1 dessertspoon strained lemon juice. Beat 1 egg yolk with 2—3 tablespoons double cream. Stir into sauce. Reheat gently without boiling. Season to taste; serve hot.

22 SOUBISE (OR ONION PURÉE) SAUCE

A smooth and creamy onion-flavoured sauce which can be served with all meat grills and roasts, boiled meats (such as beef and mutton) and grilled or fried liver. Cook 1 large onion in boiling salted water until soft. Drain and rub through a sieve (or liquidise in blender). Make up ½ pint Béchamel sauce (see Recipe 16) using all milk or half milk and half onion water. Stir in onion purée, 2 tablespoons double cream and a large pinch of nutmeg. Reheat gently without boiling. Season to taste and serve hot.

23 TARTARE SAUCE (hot)

A sauce that suits all fried fish dishes and makes a change from cold tartare sauce.

Make up ½ pint Béchamel sauce (see Recipe 16) with all milk or with half milk and half fish stock. Stir in 1 dessertspoon lemon juice, 1 level tablespoon very finely chopped parsley, 1 dessertspoon finely chopped and drained capers and 1 dessertspoon finely chopped gherkins. Beat 1 or 2 egg yolks with 2—3 tablespoons double cream. Add to sauce and reheat gently without boiling. Season to taste and serve hot.

CLASSIC VELOUTÉ SAUCE

Velouté sauce is the next classic in the white sauce category and another foundation or basic sauce from which many variations stem. It is made with clear white stock — either fish, chicken or veal — instead of milk and the flavour of the finished sauce is dependent almost entirely on the flavour of the stock used.

Because few households today have old-fashioned

stock pots, I would suggest using instead chicken stock cubes and water for poultry and veal dishes. Fish stock does have to be made with the raw materials and instructions for a very simple one are given on page 13.

Velouté sauce is also made with a roux of butter and flour which is cooked until it is the colour of light straw. (*Roux blond* to give it its correct culinary term.) It takes a little longer to cook than the white roux used for Béchamel sauce and great care must be taken to see that the butter and flour mixture is kept from darkening too much or scorching. Mushrooms are added to improve the flavour and colour, and cream is stirred in finally to enrich the sauce and to give it a creamy appearance. As the sauce requires fairly long, slow simmering, it is best made in the top of a double saucepan or in a basin standing over a saucepan of gently simmering water. This method prevents excess evaporation of liquid which occurs if the pan of sauce is cooked over direct heat.

24 VELOUTÉ SAUCE

A fine-textured sauce which may be used for fish, poultry and veal dishes.

Cooking time about 1¼ hours *Serves* 4

1 oz. butter (preferably un-salted)
1 oz. flour
½ pint cold or lukewarm fish, chicken or veal stock, depending on dish the sauce is to be served with
1 oz. mushrooms and stalks, coarsely chopped
a pinch of nutmeg
2—3 teaspoons lemon juice
2 tablespoons single cream
salt and white pepper to taste

Put butter into top of double saucepan or into an ordinary, heavy-based saucepan. Stand over low heat and leave until butter melts. Stir in flour. Cook *slowly* for about 5 minutes, stirring all the time, until roux is the colour of pale straw, not a shade darker. Remove from heat. Gradually add stock, stirring well after each addition (or add all the stock in one go). When sauce is smooth, return to medium heat. Cook, stirring with a wooden spoon all the time (or whisking with a hand whisk if liquid has been added all at once) until sauce comes to the boil and thickens. Stand top of saucepan over lower half containing gently simmering water, or transfer sauce from saucepan to basin and stand that over another saucepan of gently simmering water. Add mushrooms. Cover and cook for 1 hour, stirring occasionally. Strain through a fine sieve into a clean saucepan. Stand over a low heat. Add nutmeg and lemon juice and reheat slowly. Remove from heat and stir in cream. Season to taste and serve.

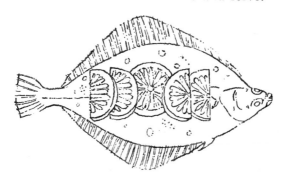

25 AURORE SAUCE

A mild, tomato-flavoured sauce with a faint blush of colour. It is pleasant with poached, grilled or steamed white fish dishes. Make up ½ pint Velouté sauce (see Recipe 24), using fish stock but omit cream. Before straining, add 2 level tablespoons tomato purée and

½ level teaspoon castor sugar. Leave sauce to cook, over hot water, for a further 10 minutes, stirring frequently. Strain. Return sauce to clean saucepan and reheat until hot. Remove from heat. Gradually add 1 oz. unsalted butter, a small piece at a time, rotating the pan gently in a circular fashion until butter melts. Do not stir and do not reheat after the butter has been added.

26 ESTRAGON SAUCE

This is basic Velouté sauce flavoured with tarragon and made with fish stock since it is essentially a sauce for poached, grilled or steamed white fish dishes. Prepare ½ pint Velouté sauce (see Recipe 24). After sauce has come to the boil and thickened, add ¼—½ level teaspoon dried tarragon. Continue to cook for required amount of time. Strain and add remaining ingredients as directed in the recipe.

27 HUNGARIAN SAUCE

A colourful sauce, particularly good with veal, poultry and fresh-water fish. Paprika itself is a mild spice and not, as many people think, hot and peppery. Consequently the sauce itself is mild and gentle despite the amount of paprika used.

Make up ½ pint Velouté sauce (see recipe 24) but omit the cream. Chop a small onion very finely. Fry slowly in 1 oz. butter until soft and just beginning to colour. Stir in 2 level tablespoons mild paprika and cook over a *very low heat* for 1 minute. A high heat and longer cooking time would give the sauce a bitter taste. Gradually add Velouté sauce, stirring all the time. Heat until hot. Remove from heat and stir in 3—4 tablespoons double cream. Season to taste.

28 NORMANDY SAUCE

An aristocratic sauce, exclusively for poached, grilled or steamed white fish dishes. It can also be served with hot lobster and crab.

Make up ½ pint Velouté sauce (see Recipe 24) with fish stock but omit cream. Beat in 1 egg yolk. Reheat gently without boiling. Remove from heat. Gradually add 1 oz. unsalted butter, a small piece at a time, rotating the pan gently in a circular fashion until the butter melts. Do not stir and do not reheat after the butter has been added.

29 RAVIGOTE SAUCE

This is a herb-flavoured sauce, served lukewarm, never hot, with platters of cold meats, poached fish of all kinds and poultry. Fresh herbs should be used whenever possible. If dried herbs only are available, then half the amount called for in the recipe should be used. Make up ½ pint Velouté sauce (see Recipe 24) but omit cream. Chop 2 shallots or 1 small onion very finely. Put into a small saucepan with 1 tablespoon of wine vinegar. Boil briskly, stirring all the time, for 3 minutes. Add Velouté sauce and simmer a further 10 minutes, stirring occasionally. Season to taste with salt and freshly milled pepper. Cool until lukewarm. Stir in 1 level tablespoon each, finely chopped parsley and chervil, 1 level dessertspoon finely chopped chives and 1 level teaspoon finely chopped tarragon.

30 SMITANE OR SOUR CREAM SAUCE

A satin-smooth, rich, creamy sauce made with soured cream which is now readily available from most supermarkets, dairies and delicatessen. It has a light and subtle piquancy and is especially good served with roast poultry, roast game birds, roast venison and grilled liver.

Make up ½ pint Velouté sauce (see Recipe 24) using chicken or veal stock. Omit cream. Finely grate 2 shallots or 1 small onion. Add 1 tablespoon wine vinegar and boil rapidly for 2 minutes. Add 4 tablespoons dry white wine and continue boiling until the liquid is reduced by half. Add Velouté sauce and simmer gently for 10 minutes, stirring all the time. Remove from heat. Gradually whisk in 1 carton (¼ pint) soured cream. Reheat without boiling. Season to taste and serve straight away.

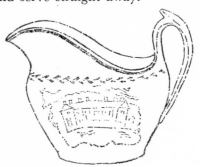

CLASSIC SUPRÊME SAUCE

This is an extension of Velouté and can be served with exactly the same dishes. Although it resembles its parent sauce fairly closely, Suprême sauce itself is richer and rounder in flavour due to the addition of egg yolks, extra cream and butter. It does require a little more attention during the final stages of preparation and, to prevent curdling and separation, care must be taken to see that the sauce is not allowed to boil after the cream and egg yolks have been added. Although

Suprême sauce is a variation of Velouté sauce, it also has its own variations and these are given after the basic recipe for Suprême sauce.

31 SUPRÊME SAUCE

Cooking time about 1 hour 20 minutes

Serves 4

½ pint freshly made Velouté sauce (without cream added)
3 tablespoons double cream

1 egg yolk
2 teaspoons lemon juice
½ oz. butter (preferably unsalted)

Pour sauce into top of double saucepan or into basin standing over pan of gently simmering water. Beat cream and egg yolk well together. Add to sauce and stir until it has thickened slightly, but on no account allow the sauce to boil or it will curdle and separate. Add lemon juice and butter and stir until butter has melted. Season to taste and serve straight away.

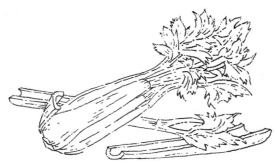

32 CELERY SAUCE

A delicate and well-flavoured sauce for poached chicken and grilled, steamed or poached fish. It also blends well with egg and cheese dishes.

Make up ½ pint Suprême sauce (see Recipe 31), but before adding cream, egg yolk, lemon juice and butter, stir in 3 level tablespoons cooked celery, finely chopped and well-drained. Use fresh or canned celery.

33 PAPRIKA SAUCE

Suprême sauce attractively tinted pale pink with paprika. Serve with the same dishes as Velouté.

Make up ½ pint Suprême sauce. Before adding unsalted butter at the end, cream the butter first with ¼—½ level teaspoon paprika.

34 POULETTE SAUCE

Suprême sauce with the merest hint of chopped parsley. It is especially good with chicken, calves' liver, veal and all poached, grilled or steamed white fish dishes.

Make up ½ pint Suprême sauce (see Recipe 31), but stir in 2 level teaspoons finely chopped parsley with lemon juice and butter.

35 ALLEMANDE SAUCE

An even creamier and richer sauce than Suprême but otherwise very similar in character. Usually served with poached chicken, poached white fish, cauliflower and broccoli. I often serve the sauce over tiny new potatoes and baby carrots; it makes a change from butter! It is also delicious served with marrow. Allemande sauce has a few variations of its own and these are given after the basic recipe.

Make up ½ pint Suprême sauce (see Recipe 31) but use 3 egg yolks and 4 tablespoons double cream.

36 FLAMANDE SAUCE

This is Allemande sauce lightly flavoured with mustard.
It is luxurious with hot lobster, crab and scampi,
grilled or baked ham, roast rabbit or boiled beef.

Make up ½ pint Allemande sauce (see Recipe 35),
but before adding cream, egg yolks, lemon juice and
butter, gently whisk in 1 level teaspoon made English
mustard (mild) or 1 level teaspoon French mustard.

37 NIVERNAISE SAUCE

A pretty and colourful sauce containing thin shreds of
carrots. Suitable for poultry, veal and egg dishes.

Make up ½ pint Allemande sauce (see Recipe 35)
but before adding cream, egg yolks, lemon juice and
butter, stir in 3—4 level tablespoons of cooked carrots
cut into thin strips (or finely grated).

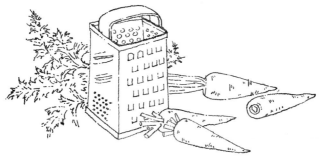

38 PRINCESSE SAUCE

A luxury version of Mushroom sauce for white
fish dishes, egg dishes and for poultry and rabbit.

Make up ½ pint Allemande sauce (see Recipe 35)
but before adding cream, egg yolks, lemon juice and
butter, stir in 3 oz. thinly sliced mushrooms, gently
poached in milk for 2 or 3 minutes and then drained.

Classic Brown Sauces

A sweet meat must have sour sauce

A Victorian encyclopedia of cookery says this: 'In common parlance and in the chief dictionaries, gravy always means the juice of roasted meat; in the kitchen and in many cookery books, it has been found necessary to extend its meaning to the juice of meat however obtained whether from roasting or decoction. The word sauce in its origin is always a doublet of salt, in its modern use it nearly always implies a liquid, and it may be defined in the most general terms as any liquid seasoning employed in the presentation of food. Gravy or the juice of meat is always a sauce, although a sauce is not always a gravy. On the other hand the great sauces, as they are called in France, have gravy for their foundation, this too in its most concentrated form, and it would be more descriptive to call them, at least in England, gravies.'

Thus the Sunday lunch gravy as we know it in England is the most basic, the most unsophisticated and the most uncomplicated of all the brown sauces and the one which, through sheer popularity, is made more frequently than almost any other. It owes its full, round flavour, smooth pouring consistency, bright gloss and unique character to the meat or poultry juices left behind in the roasting tin and to the subsequent additions of flour or cornflour, fat-free stock or water and seasonings. With no further adornments it is in fact, Demi-glace (or Half-glaze) sauce, the very finest of all the Classic Brown Sauces.

These days, alas, meat is dearer than it was in Queen Victoria's day. We eat it less frequently and so dark brown jellied meat juices, in any quantity, are hard to come by and home-made bone stock is no easier. Thus we compromise, through necessity rather than choice, and turn to ingredients which are more readily available such as stock cubes and water instead of home-cooked stock; bacon and sometimes meat extract for flavour; tomato purée or paste and fresh tomatoes for colour.

We start with Espagnole sauce which, when simmered with an equal amount of good gravy, makes a fair substitute for one of the most highly esteemed sauces of all — the Demi-glace. But first things first. Espagnole sauce is the most important one in the brown repertoire and like its white and blond counterparts, is a sauce from which many variations spring. It is made, like the other flour-thickened sauces, with a roux of fat and flour plus vegetables and spices for extra flavour and colour. As the sauce should reflect faithfully the dish with which it is to be served, the stock itself is very important and ideally one should use lamb stock for lamb dishes, beef stock for beef dishes, game stock for game dishes and so on. Since this is not always possible, a few tablespoons of jellied meat juices (left-over from roasting a joint of meat and usually found under the hard layer of fat in a bowl of dripping) can be added to the sauce to give it an authentic flavour. This is not essential and whether you do so or not must be left to personal taste.

Espagnole sauce is made, as I said earlier, with a roux but this time the fat, which can be olive or corn oil, butter and/or good quality pork or beef dripping, is cooked with the flour until it turns a warm brown (roux brun). This roux, together with fried vegetables and bacon, is responsible for giving the sauce its characteristic brown colour. Without it, the sauce would need to be artificially coloured with something like gravy browning. It is difficult to say exactly how long the roux should take to turn brown, but in general terms it should be kept over a low heat all the time and watched carefully after 4 minutes. When it starts to brown, it does so fairly rapidly and, if left unwatched, the roux could burn with surprising speed. Once the stock has been added, the sauce needs to cook for approximately 45 minutes—1 hour.

Evaporation will inevitably take place if the pan of sauce is over direct heat, so here are a few alternatives which will stop the sauce boiling away to nothing. Either cook the sauce in a pan with a thick, heavy base; stand an asbestos mat between the pan and the source of heat; cook the sauce in a basin standing over a saucepan of gently simmering water, or pour the sauce into a casserole dish, cover it with a lid or piece of aluminium foil and let it cook in the centre of a moderate oven for approximately 2 hours. If the sauce is cooked in a saucepan, stir it frequently.

Seasoning is another thing which requires care. Bearing in mind the possibility of evaporation and the fact that bacon itself and the stock both contain salt, it is safer to add no seasoning to the sauce until after it has been cooked and strained. While an under-seasoned sauce would be a disappointing anti-climax, an over-seasoned one would, for many people, spell ruination! A greasy brown sauce is not only indigestible, but looks unappetising and unpalatable. Therefore the fat should be skimmed off.

Espagnole is a well-flavoured brown sauce which can be served with meat grills and roasts, offal (such as liver and tongue), game and pork or beef sausages. It can also be used in a Shepherd's Pie instead of gravy. As Espagnole sauce will keep a minimum of a week in the refrigerator, it is a good idea to make double or even treble the quantity given in the recipe, so that you have a store of prepared sauce ready to be reheated and served as it is or turned into any number of variations. To store the sauce, transfer it to a bowl and pour over a thin layer of butter or dripping which will harden in the refrigerator and form a lid. Espagnole sauce can be frozen in the same way as Béchamel sauce. For instructions, see page 19.

I will shortly give the classic recipe and method for Espagnole sauce but before doing so, would like to give an alternative method which some people may find easier. This version does not use a roux. Instead, the bacon and vegetables are fried slowly until golden brown in the butter, oil or dripping (or mixture). The stock is added with the remaining ingredients and the sauce is then simmered for 45 minutes—1 hour. After straining, it is poured into a measuring cup and made up to ½ pint with extra stock. It is then returned to a clean saucepan. Added to it is 1 oz. cornflour mixed to a smooth cream with 3 tablespoons of cold water. The sauce is then brought to the boil (it must be stirred continuously), simmered for 5 minutes and skimmed of excess fat. Prepared this way, with the thickening taking place at the very end, the sauce will not stick and burn while it is simmering and consequently will not require much attention in the way of stirring. Also, it will have a very high gloss.

The major disadvantages are these: the sauce may be insufficiently brown without a roux, and gravy browning may therefore have to be added. The flavour may lack something of the roundness usually found in an Espagnole sauce made in the traditional manner. Which method to use is again a matter of personal taste, but I would recommend making both versions and then seeing which you prefer.

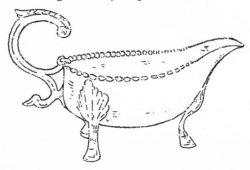

Home-made jellied stock for brown sauces. For the purists who care enough and who have time enough and who seek perfection, I give below a simple method of making stock which is vastly superior to modern substitutes.

You need a good veal bone, part of the shin or the knuckle. Put it into a large saucepan containing 4 pints of cold water. Add 1 lb. shin of beef (this can be kept and used later for shepherd's pies or any other dish calling for cooked boiled beef), a sprig of parsley, 2 large onions, 2 carrots and 2 oz. bacon scraps. Bring to the boil and remove scum. Add no further seasonings at all as the stock will become over salty if you do. Cover the pan and simmer the contents gently for 5—6 hours. Transfer to a large dish or bowl and stand it in a cool place overnight.

Remove layer of fat from the top and underneath you should be left with a lightly jellied stock, perfect for any brown sauce. If you prefer to concentrate this stock still further, simmer it gently until it becomes as syrupy and as glossy as black treacle. A few tablespoons can then be added to any brown sauce to improve its flavour. The stock will keep perfectly well in the refrigerator for a week or so covered with either a layer of melted fat or a piece of aluminium foil.

As an alternative, you might like to try this recipe from an early Mrs. Beeton where the word gravy seems to be used instead of stock and where economy appears to have been as important then as it is now.

'The general basis of most gravies and some sauces is the same stock as that used for soups and, by the employment of those, with perhaps an additional slice of ham, a little spice, a few herbs, and a slight flavouring from some cold sauce or ketchup, very nice gravies may be made for a very small expenditure. A milt (either of a bullock or sheep), the shank-end of mutton that has already been dressed, and the necks and feet of poultry, may all be advantageously used for gravy, where much is not required. It may, then, be established as a rule, that there exists no necessity for good gravies to be expensive, and that there is no occasion, as many would have the world believe, to buy many pounds of fresh meat in order to furnish a little quantity of gravy.'

39 ESPAGNOLE (OR BROWN) SAUCE

Cooking time 1¼ hours   *Serves 4*

1 oz. lean bacon (or bacon trimmings)
1 medium onion, chopped
1 small celery stalk
1 oz. mushrooms
1 small carrot
1 oz. unsalted butter or dripping or 3 dessert-spoons oil (or mixture)
¾ oz. flour
½ pint meat stock (stock cube and water)

2 level teaspoons tomato purée or paste
1 medium tomato, skinned
1 bay leaf
2 level tablespoons coarsely chopped parsley
2 black peppercorns
2 tablespoons jellied meat juice (optional)
salt and pepper to taste

Coarsely chop bacon, onion, celery and mushrooms. Slice carrot fairly thickly. Melt butter, dripping or oil (or mixture) in a saucepan. When hot and sizzling, add bacon and chopped vegetables. Cover and fry 10 minutes, shaking pan frequently. Remove lid and continue to fry until bacon and vegetables are pale gold. Stir in flour and cook over a low heat, stirring continuously, until the roux turns a deep golden brown.

Remove from heat. Gradually stir in stock. Return to heat. Cook, stirring with a spoon all the time, until sauce comes to the boil and thickens. Add all remaining ingredients except salt and pepper. Cover and simmer gently, as described in the introduction to this section (see page 34) for 45 minutes—1 hour. Stir frequently and skim off fat as it rises to the top. Alternatively, transfer the sauce to a casserole dish with a lid and cook in the centre of a moderate oven for 2 hours. Strain the cooked and fat-skimmed sauce into a pan and adjust seasoning. Reheat before serving.

40 BORDELAISE SAUCE

A fine-tasting sauce flavoured with red wine, shallots or onion and a hint of herbs. A perfect partner for grilled chops and steaks, breaded and fried sweetbreads and grilled kidneys.

Make up ½ pint Espagnole sauce (see Recipe 39). Put 6 tablespoons dry red wine into a saucepan. Add 1 finely chopped shallot or ½ a small onion. Boil until reduced by half. Add Espagnole sauce and a pinch of dried tarragon and thyme. Simmer for 10 minutes. Strain and adjust seasoning to taste. Just before serving, reheat the sauce then add a squeeze of lemon and 1 level dessertspoon of finely chopped parsley.

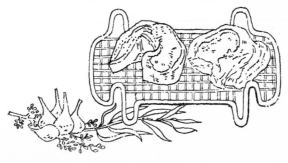

41 CHASSEUR SAUCE

Also known as Hunters' sauce. It is a robust, full-flavoured and colourful sauce; slightly extravagant if brandy is added; less so if it isn't. It is usually served with grilled meats, roast joints and some entrées. I like it with roast duck, lightly fried calves' liver and grilled gammon steaks.

Make up ½ pint Espagnole sauce (see Recipe 39). Chop finely 1 small onion or shallot and fry gently in 1 oz. butter until soft but not brown. Chop coarsely 3 oz. mushrooms, add to pan and fry slowly for 2—3 minutes. Add 5 tablespoons dry white wine or 3 tablespoons wine and 2 tablespoons brandy. Stir in 1 tablespoon tomato purée and the Espagnole sauce. Simmer gently for 5—6 minutes. Season to taste and stir in 2 level teaspoons chopped parsley just before serving.

42 MARCHAND DE VIN SAUCE

A beautiful sauce with a fine bouquet. Eminently suitable for serving with grilled beef or gammon steaks, roast duck, goose or pork, hot boiled tongue and stuffed roast heart.

Make up ½ pint Espagnole sauce (see Recipe 39). Chop finely 1 small onion or shallot. Fry gently in 1 oz. butter until soft but not brown. Chop coarsely 4 oz. mushrooms. Add to pan and fry slowly for 2—3 minutes. Stir in ¼ pint beef stock (use stock cube and water if home-cooked stock is not available) and simmer for 15 minutes. Add Espagnole sauce and 6 tablespoons dry red wine. Simmer, uncovered, for 20 minutes. Season to taste then add juice of 1 lemon.

43 PIQUANT SAUCE

A tangy, strong-flavoured sauce which adds piquancy and zest to any foods with which it is served. It goes particularly well with meat cutlets and croquettes, with cold roast meats, hot roast pork, or boiled bacon.

Make up ½ pint Espagnole sauce (see Recipe 39). Gently fry 1 small chopped onion or shallot in 1 oz. butter until soft but not brown. Add 3 tablespoons wine vinegar. Boil until reduced by half. Stir in Espagnole sauce and simmer for 15 minutes. Add 1 level dessert-spoon chopped capers, 3 finely chopped gherkins, and 1 level tablespoon chopped parsley. Season to taste and reheat for 5 minutes.

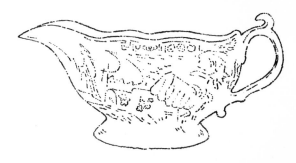

44 ROBERT SAUCE

A long established and well-known sauce of the great family of brown classics. It is lightly flavoured with dry white wine and Dijon mustard and is extremely good with cold roast meat and poultry, with roast goose and pork, with venison and with hot boiled beef and tongue.

Make up ½ pint of Espagnole sauce (see Recipe 39). Gently fry 1 large chopped onion in 1 oz. butter until soft but not brown. Add 4 tablespoons dry white wine and 2 tablespoons of vinegar. Boil until reduced by half. Add Espagnole sauce and simmer for 20 minutes. Stir in 2 level teaspoons Dijon mustard and a pinch of sugar. Season to taste.

45 CHARCUTIÈRE SAUCE

This is simply Robert sauce (see Recipe 44) with 6 small chopped gherkins stirred in at the end. It can be served with all red meat dishes although it is usually made to accompany entrées.

46 LYONNAISE SAUCE

A good-tasting brown sauce, well endowed with butter-fried onions. Its best partners are grilled or fried liver, beef dishes and roast pork.

Make up $\frac{1}{2}$ pint Espagnole sauce (see Recipe 39). Cut 1 large onion into thin slices then separate into rings. Fry slowly in $1-1\frac{1}{2}$ oz. of butter until they are pale gold. Add to sauce and season to taste.

47 POIVRADE OR PEPPER SAUCE

A full-bodied and peppery sauce, traditionally served with venison but also popular with grilled steaks, with beef roasts and with other game such as hare.

Make up ½ pint Espagnole sauce (see Recipe 39). Then chop 1 small onion and put into a saucepan. Add ¼ pint wine vinegar and 3 tablespoons dry red wine. Boil until reduced by half. Stir in Espagnole sauce and simmer for 20 minutes. Add 8 crushed or coarsely ground peppercorns and simmer a further 5 minutes. Strain and add sufficient freshly ground black pepper to make the sauce hot. Reheat gently before serving.

48 DIANE SAUCE

A mellow version of Poivrade sauce, enriched with cream and suitable for exactly the same dishes.

Make up ½ pint Poivrade sauce (see Recipe 47). After straining, add 4—5 tablespoons of double cream and sufficient freshly ground pepper to make the sauce hot. Reheat gently without boiling.

49 REFORM SAUCE

Named after the club at which it was first introduced by the well-known chef, Alexis Soyer, over 100 years ago. Traditionally the sauce should contain chopped white of egg, gherkin, cooked tongue, truffles, port and redcurrant jelly, but nowadays a simpler version is made and the true character of the sauce is, regrettably, lost to some extent. The recipe I give is a slight compromise between the two — the old and the new — and uses pickled walnuts or cooked beetroot instead of the very costly and hard to find truffles. Reform sauce was originally created especially for lamb cutlets but it goes equally well with grilled pork chops or steak.

Make up ½ pint Poivrade sauce (see Recipe 47). After straining, stir in 4 tablespoons port and 1 tablespoon redcurrant jelly. Simmer very slowly, uncovered, for 15 minutes. Cut into match-stick-sized strips, 1 egg white, 1 gherkin, 1 oz. cooked tongue, 2 raw mushrooms and 1 truffle (or ½ a pickled walnut or 1 slice of beetroot). Add to sauce and heat through gently. Season.

50 DEMI-GLACE SAUCE

A great sauce that is no harder to produce than the Espagnole. Strictly speaking, it should be made with jellied meat juices and little else, but a similar sauce can be made by combining Espagnole sauce with good, concentrated beef stock, home-cooked for preference. If this is not possible, beef stock cubes and water may be used instead, but to improve the flavour 1 or 2 tablespoons of jellied meat juices (from the weekend joint) or 1 or 2 teaspoons of meat extract should be added as well. Demi-glace sauce can be served with all red meat dishes and game.

Put ½ pint Espagnole sauce (see Recipe 39) into a heavy-based saucepan. Add ½ pint home-made meat stock (or stock cubes and water plus 1 or 2 tablespoons jellied meat juices or 1 or 2 teaspoons meat extract). Simmer slowly, uncovered, until sauce is reduced by half. Strain and return to a clean saucepan. Leave over a low heat and stir in 3 dessertspoons of dry sherry. Reheat without boiling and season to taste.

51 BIGARADE (OR ORANGE) SAUCE

A sophisticated brown sauce, flavoured with orange and lemon juice and port. Fine shreds of orange rind add to its taste and it is especially recommended for duck, goose and all game dishes.

Make up ½ pint Demi-glace sauce (see Recipe 50) but omit the sherry. After straining, stir in the juice of 1 small lemon and 1 small orange, 1 level tablespoon finely shredded orange rind and 3 tablespoons dry red wine. Reheat gently without boiling and season.

52 MADEIRA SAUCE

One of the greatest classics of all time. It is perfect with hot tongue, game dishes and fillet of beef.

Make up ½ pint Demi-glace (sauce see Recipe 50) but omit the sherry. After straining, stir in 5—8 tablespoons Madeira wine. Reheat gently without boiling and season to taste.

53 PÉRIGUEUX SAUCE

A luxurious sauce containing port and truffles. It is exquisite with meat cutlets, meat croquettes, and roast chicken — and surprisingly enough with omelettes.

Make up ½ pint Madeira sauce (see Recipe 52). Stir in 1 tablespoon finely chopped truffles. Season to taste.

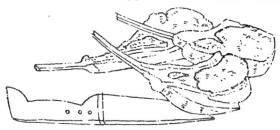

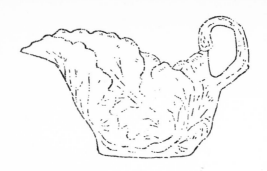

Egg-Based Sauces

Dexterity comes by experience

Hollandaise Sauce is the bright shining star of the show — regal — temperamental — unpredictable — often exasperating unless handled with care and understanding. Hollandaise Sauce expects to be treated with all the pomp and all the circumstance usually reserved for great prima donnas. Do so, and she will reward you with one of those dazzling and memorable performances that have made her world renowned.

Hollandaise is a delicate, golden-hearted and glowingly rich sauce made from egg yolks, acid (in the form of lemon juice and/or vinegar) and always butter. Some consider it to be one of the most difficult sauces to make well and consequently more has been written about it than about almost any other sauce in existence.

There are the traditionalists who believe no true Hollandaise should ever contain vinegar, only lemon juice. Others claim no vinegar and all lemon juice makes Hollandaise a dull sauce. Others maintain the butter must always be clarified. Some regard this as unnecessary. Whether the butter should be salted or unsalted is a debatable point too, but in general most experts agree that the butter should be unsalted. Some cooks heat the vinegar or lemon juice (or both) with peppercorns and a bay leaf for extra flavour. Others add no flavouring at all other than salt and pepper. Some cook it over direct heat like an egg custard. Others always use a double saucepan or basin over hot water. Some say you should never use a metal whisk for whisking the sauce because it discolours it. Others wouldn't use anything else. There are so many opposing views that it is hard to know what is right and which is best. In the end I tried out all the different ways and means of Hollandaise and give later those that worked best for me, plus the traditional recipe.

Although a well-made Hollandaise is one of the most pleasurable and superb sauces of all it can, equally, be an utter flop and failure if it is badly or carelessly made. Nothing looks quite as sad, or causes such a feeling of disappointment, as a Hollandaise sauce which has separated out into curds and whey just as you're about to serve the best meal of your life to a group of very important dinner guests! You fume and you rave and you rant (quietly, so that no one can hear you!) wondering why and where you went wrong and what you can do at the very last moment to put things right.

You probably let the sauce get too hot so that it boiled and curdled; or you used melted butter and added it before it had cooled sufficiently; or you didn't melt the butter and added large pieces of it too quickly; or you chose a close and humid day and didn't clarify the butter first (for some reason humidity and unclarified butter react badly on a Hollandaise sauce); or you didn't stir enough. A good many reasons for the sauce going wrong you'll agree!

The procedure is this and the same principles apply whichever version of Hollandaise sauce you choose to make: the sauce contains four main ingredients — egg yolks, water, acid and butter, plus seasoning. In order to hold together sufficiently to form a sauce and coat food, the ingredients have to be cooked like an egg custard. *Slowly and gently.* The egg yolks should be the same temperature as the kitchen. The water and acid should be just luke-warm, certainly no hotter, although one recipe I give does call for boiling water and another for boiling lemon juice. If the recipe is the one using melted butter, then the butter must be left until it is luke-warm; not hot and not forgotten about until it's cold and congealed.

On a sultry summer day clarify the butter first and directions for how to do it are give in the Butter Sauces section on page 77. The four main ingredients should be cooked in a glass or china-type pudding basin over a saucepan of hot (never boiling) water or in the top of a double saucepan, enamel preferably, as aluminium is inclined to give the sauce a greenish tinge. The sauce should be whisked gently all the time with a balloon whisk or, even better, with one of those Scandinavian whisks that are made from fine twigs. Another implement I find useful for whisking is a wooden fork — part of a set of salad servers.

As soon as the sauce has thickened and is smooth, take the basin away from the hot water to stop the sauce from cooking any further. If it is allowed to overcook, it may thicken up too much or get overheated and curdle. Serve it at once or leave it in a vacuum flask until needed. If, despite all the care and all the attention, your Hollandaise sauce still separates, try beating in 2 tablespoons double cream. Or tip the sauce into the liquidiser and blend until it is smooth. As a last resort, put a fresh egg yolk into a basin over hot water and very slowly and very gradually beat the curdled Hollandaise sauce into it. There is no remedy if the eggs have overcooked to such an extent that they are scrambled!

Hollandaise sauce should always be served luke-warm with poached salmon, salmon trout, with poached sole, halibut or turbot, with chicken, with broccoli, asparagus, and globe artichokes. It is heavenly with avocado pears for those who can take superlatively rich food and aren't worried about calories!

54 HOLLANDAISE SAUCE (1)

This is the traditional Hollandaise sauce, made as the purists would make it. In this recipe the vinegar, lemon juice and water are first reduced by boiling, and the butter is not melted but softened and added in small pieces.

Cooking time 10—15 minutes *Serves* 4—6

4 oz. unsalted butter, softened	2 extra teaspoons cold water
2 tablespoons lemon juice	3 egg yolks
2 tablespoons wine vinegar	salt and pepper to taste
1 tablespoon water	pinch of sugar (optional)

Cut butter into 8 or 9 pieces. Put lemon juice, vinegar and water into a small saucepan. Boil briskly until the mixture is well reduced and only 2 tablespoons remain. Stir in 2 teaspoons cold water. Put into the top of a double saucepan or into a glass or china-type pudding basin. Stand over a pan containing water that is just hot enough to tremble gently; it must *not* be boiling. Add egg yolks. Stand over low heat and whisk until egg yolks begin to thicken. Add one portion of butter. Whisk until it has melted. Add next portion of butter and continue whisking until it, too, has melted. Add portion after portion of butter until all the butter has been incorporated into the sauce and the sauce itself is thick enough to coat the back of a spoon. If it thickens up too much, add 1 or 2 teaspoons cold water and make sure that the water over which the sauce is standing never boils. Season to taste with salt and pepper, and if liked, a pinch of castor sugar.

If preferred, all lemon juice may be used instead of vinegar. Put 2 tablespoons lemon juice into the pan with 2 tablespoons water. Boil briskly until only 2 tablespoons remain.

55 HOLLANDAISE SAUCE (2)

In this version there is no reduction of lemon juice and water and the butter is melted first before it is added. I find this easier to make than Hollandaise Sauce (1) and provided the temperature of the water in the saucepan over which the sauce is cooking is watched carefully and never allowed to boil, there should be no problems with the sauce itself. When I first tried this method I had doubts, but it worked perfectly and I've been making Hollandaise sauce this way ever since.

Cooking time 15 minutes   *Serves* 4—6

4 oz. unsalted butter	1 tablespoon lemon juice
3 egg yolks	$\frac{1}{4}$ level teaspoon sugar
3 tablespoons boiling water	salt and pepper to taste
1 tablespoon wine vinegar	

Melt the butter and leave on one side until luke-warm. Put egg yolks into the top of a double saucepan or into a glass or china-type pudding basin. Stand over gently simmering water. Add 1 tablespoon boiling water and whisk until yolks begin to thicken. Add a second tablespoon of boiling water and whisk until yolks thicken again. Repeat using last tablespoon of boiling water. Heat the vinegar and lemon juice until they are luke-warm. Beat into egg yolks. Still whisking continuously, start adding half the melted butter, a teaspoon at a time. When the sauce is thick and fluffy, add the remaining butter in a slow, continuous stream, whisking all the time. If the sauce appears to be rather thin, slightly increase heat under saucepan of water; it is possible that the water is not hot enough to cook the egg yolks and consequently thicken the sauce. If the sauce becomes too thick, add 1 or 2 teaspoons cold water. Add sugar and season to taste with salt and pepper. Serve straight away.

56 HOLLANDAISE SAUCE (3)

This method may cause many people to shudder; Hollandaise sauce cooked over direct heat, instead of being gently nursed over hot water! However, if care is taken it works perfectly well, and is certainly a short-cut method. The thing here is to choose a saucepan with a thick, heavy base and to keep the heat as low as possible underneath it. A hand whisk is also desirable; it is more reliable than a spoon.

Cooking time 7—10 minutes   *Serves* 4—6

4 oz. unsalted butter	1 tablespoon vinegar
2 egg yolks	1 tablespoon lemon juice
1 tablespoon water	salt and pepper

Melt butter and leave until luke-warm. Put egg yolks into a saucepan with water, vinegar and lemon juice. Stand over a low heat and whisk until mixture begins to thicken. Add half the butter, a teaspoon at a time, whisking continuously all the while. When the sauce has thickened and clearly isn't going to separate out and curdle, add rest of butter in a slow trickle, still whisking all the time. Remove from heat. Season to taste with salt and pepper and pour sauce into a sauce-boat or jug straight away; if the sauce were left in the pan, the heat of the metal would over-cook it.

57 HOLLANDAISE SAUCE (4)

For those with blenders, this easy Hollandaise sauce works like a dream and can literally be made in seconds. It hasn't quite the same lightness as a hand-made Hollandaise, but one can forgive it this single weakness in view of its excellent flavour and consistency and the speed with which it can be made.

Cooking time 2 minutes   *Serves* 4

6 oz. melted butter	pinch castor sugar
2 tablespoons lemon juice	$\frac{1}{4}$ level teaspoon salt
3 egg yolks	shake of white pepper

Put butter into a pan and stand over a low heat until it is hot and foaming. Bring lemon juice just up to the boil. Put egg yolks into blender with sugar, salt and pepper and boiling lemon juice. Blend for 6 seconds. Remove lid and with blender set to high speed, add the hot butter in a steady stream. The sauce should be thick and smooth within 35—40 seconds. If it is too thick, add 1 or 2 teaspoons hot water. Serve straight away.

Like all the other sauces, Hollandaise sauce also has its own variations and these are listed below. Any of the Hollandaise sauce recipes given may be used.

58 BAVAROISE SAUCE

A sauce lightly flavoured with horseradish. It excels with trout and mackerel dishes and cold roast beef and tongue. Make up any one of the recipes given for Hollandaise sauce. Just before serving, stir in 2 level teaspoons horseradish sauce.

59 BÉARNAISE SAUCE

The great and celebrated Béarnaise sauce is stated, by some authorities, to have come from the Béarnaise region of France — hence its name. Others claim it has no connection with Béarn whatever but was created by a chef of the Pavillon Henry IV near Paris in about 1835. No one knows the true story, but all connoisseurs of good eating agree that this is one of the most exquisitely flavoured sauces there is and have nothing but praise and admiration for its creator, whoever he was and wherever he came from. Béarnaise sauce is traditionally served with grilled steaks, but it is also excellent with thick underdone slices of roast beef, grilled kidneys, poached fish and egg dishes.

Put 4 tablespoons dry white wine, 2 tablespoons tarragon vinegar, 1 small finely chopped onion and 1 parsley sprig into a small saucepan. Boil briskly until mixture is well reduced and only 2 tablespoons remain. Strain and stir in 2 teaspoons warm water. Make up any one of Hollandaise sauce recipes using this tarragon flavoured liquor instead of the lemon juice and/or vinegar. Just before serving, stir in a large pinch of dried tarragon or finely chopped fresh tarragon.

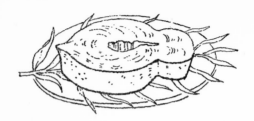

60 CHORON SAUCE

This is Béarnaise sauce tinted and flavoured with tomato purée. It is well-coloured and tastes impressive with grilled steaks, poached salmon or egg dishes.

Make up the Béarnaise sauce recipe (see Recipe 59). Just before serving, stir in 2 level tablespoons tomato purée with the tarragon.

61 FOYOT SAUCE

This is another variation of Béarnaise sauce, but jellied meat juices are added to strengthen the flavour. It is a sauce that must be kept exclusively for meat.

Make up the Béarnaise sauce recipe (see Recipe 59). Just before serving, stir in 2 tablespoons jellied meat juices, heated through until luke-warm.

62 MALTESE SAUCE

Hollandaise sauce fragrant with orange. Blood oranges are the traditional ones to use, but as these are not generally available all the year round, any other type of orange may be used instead. The sauce is generally served with asparagus or broccoli but it is worth trying with poached sole or plaice and veal dishes.

Make up any one of the recipes give for Hollandaise sauce. Just before serving, stir in 2 tablespoons strained and warmed orange juice and 1 level teaspoon finely grated orange peel.

63 MEDICI SAUCE

Another version of Béarnaise sauce, flavoured with port and tomato purée. This is a man's sauce again for serving with thick, underdone steaks and roast beef.

Make up the Béarnaise sauce recipe (see Recipe 59). Just before serving, stir in 1 tablespoon luke-warm port mixed with 1 level tablespoon tomato purée.

64 MOUSSELINE SAUCE

Hollandaise sauce enriched with softly whipped cream. It is a luxurious and sumptuous affair and a gladsome thing to serve with light-as-air soufflés, salmon and salmon trout, poached white fish dishes, asparagus, broccoli, globe artichokes and chicken.

Make up any one of the recipes given for Hollandaise sauce. Just before serving, stir in 3—4 tablespoons softly whipped cream.

65 PALOIS SAUCE

This is very similar to Béarnaise sauce except that mint is used instead of tarragon. The flavour is mild and subtle and the sauce is particularly recommended for serving with roast and grilled lamb, roast mutton, roast and grilled chicken and turkey.

Make up the Béarnaise sauce recipe as given, but use wine vinegar instead of tarragon vinegar. Add 3—4 leaves of fresh mint (or 1 level teaspoon dried mint) to the wine mixture before reducing it by boiling. Just before serving the sauce, stir in 1 level teaspoon finely chopped fresh mint or $\frac{1}{4}$ level teaspoon dried mint.

MAYONNAISE

Home-made mayonnaise is habit forming. Taste it once and you're an addict for life! I was brought up, like most of us, on the bottled kind and loved it — until I at last tasted the real thing. Many years ago a friend and I were holidaying in the Loire region of France. Like most young students, we had comparatively little money so most of our meals were alfresco style — bread, cheese (soft and melting and gloriously smelly!) and wine — eaten along the wayside or in our tiny attic room when the weather was too wet or too cold to picnic. On our last day we gathered together what few remaining francs we had and made up our minds to splash out on a really first-class lunch, provided it was cheap. Luckily we found a restaurant, at our price, tucked away in a narrow back street. It had a very ordinary appearance from the outside, but inside it looked exactly as one always imagines a French country restaurant should look. There were scrubbed wooden tables brightly topped with red and white gingham squares; there were busy and bustling waitresses, bearing outsize trays of food with remarkable good cheer; there were all the lunch-time locals busily eating away with obvious dedication!

We started the meal with a salad made from those huge scarlet tomatoes, juicy and sweet and smothered with parsley and chopped onion. Then came the next course and *voilà* — mayonnaise entered my life! It was covering a liberal serving of cold fish salad and didn't, I admit, look in the least bit special. Then I tasted it and that was my undoing! What a magnificent flavour that dish had. To me, young and with no real knowledge of classical cooking, it was a revelation, a unique and memorable experience and I have never forgotten the glorious taste of that unadorned mayonnaise sauce and how it turned what was a very mundane piece of fish into a meal fit for the gods. If the years have made me blasé over other things, the magical quality of real mayonnaise still remains, despite its familiarity. It may have substitutes but it has no equal on this earth.

Mayonnaise is a centuries-old sauce with a good deal of historical controversy associated with it. Did it originate in Provence? Or in Spain? No one can be certain although it is assumed now that it must have started life in one of the olive growing areas of the Mediterranean. As it was once called Mahonaise —

after Port Mahon in Minorca where the British were defeated by the French some two hundred years ago — it seems highly probable that it is of Spanish descent. On the other hand, 'The Best of Everything', a book of all-sorts published round about 1870 refers to it as a French receipt and the great Carême must have considered it to be French, since he called it *Magnonaise*, from the verb *manier*, meaning to stir.

Another story, which may be fact or fancy, says that mayonnaise is really *Moyeunaise*, from the old French word *moyeu*, meaning an egg yolk, but my Victorian encyclopedia gives the most whimsical explanation of all. It is this: 'It is mis-spelled. It should be Mahonnaise, from an old Provençal word, signifying a lady who fatigues, or thoroughly mixes a salad. At one time it was usual for the youngest and prettiest of the ladies to mix the salad and fatigue it with her dainty fingers. Hence it came to pass that the salad or its dressing was called by the word denoting the operator. This is a very unsatisfactory explanation but none better presents itself.' After all this we are none the wiser! What we do know is that mayonnaise, Mahonnaise, Magnonaise, Moyeunaise or Mahonnaise, which has oil in it as its main ingredient, is the only sauce of coating consistency which requires no cooking.

Mayonnaise is a thick emulsion of egg yolks, oil and acid and, to quote an early Mrs. Beeton, 'patience and practice, let us add, are two essentials for making this sauce good'. It is not a particularly difficult sauce to make but it will play tricks if some of the processes are hurried; there are no short cuts (unless one uses a blender) where a legitimate and traditional mayonnaise is concerned and it is as well to accept this.

Although mayonnaise has a basic recipe in the same way as all other sauces, no two cookery books, or cooks for that matter, give the identical recipe, largely because additions vary according to who is making the sauce. Some people like French mustard, others English. Some people add Worcestershire sauce, others don't. Some add only lemon juice, others a mixture of lemon juice and vinegar. Some cooks (as I do) add a pinch of sugar to take away the acid tang, others would regard this as being over-fussy. Some cooks use olive oil, some use corn oil, some use groundnut oil, others still use a mixture of oils. Some add boiling water at the end to prevent the mayonnaise from separating after it has been standing for a few days, others regard this as a waste of time. And so it goes on, individual touches all round.

It seems the most controversial issue of all is the oil. In the world of *haute cuisine* olive oil — which dates back to the Old Testament — is always used. And it has to be the purest and the finest; the 'virgin oil' which comes from the first pressing of the ripe, delicate olives. To others, the distinctive, almost nutty flavour of olive oil is too rich and over-powering. They prefer the blander taste of corn or groundnut oil.

I have made mayonnaise with all the different oils and the one which pleases me most is the one where I use half groundnut or corn oil and half olive oil. It satisfies the purists who would normally criticise a mayonnaise without olive oil and it satisfies the non-purists who would, with equal vehemence, criticise a mayonnaise made with all olive oil. Most important, it satisfies me!

Vinegar versus lemon juice — I know not the answer! Again personal taste must enter into this argument. Those who like mayonnaise with angelic mildness will use lemon juice only. Those who like mayonnaise with a bit more kick, will reach for the vinegar bottle instead of, or in addition to, the lemon juice. What I must add here is that malt vinegar is too hard and too brittle for mayonnaise; it has to be the finest and the best quality wine or cider vinegar only.

I cannot be too adamant about the mustard either. It can be English or it can be Continental; either French or German. The flavours of these mustards are so distinctive and so completely different that the choice has to be left to you.

The secret of good mayonnaise depends on the temperature of the ingredients, the proportion of oil to egg yolks and the way in which the oil is added to the egg yolks and seasonings. The yolks and oil should be the same temperature as the kitchen. If any of these ingredients are cold such as an egg yolk taken straight from the refrigerator or a chilled bottle of oil, it could give trouble and cause the mayonnaise to curdle; the only major disaster that could happen and the one which everyone strives to avoid.

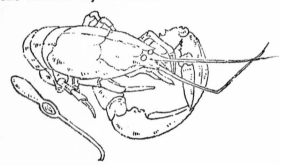

The proportion of egg yolks to oil is important too because the more yolks you use, the less chance there will be of the sauce curdling. The recommended proportion is 2 egg yolks to every ½ pint of oil, but beginners will find that 3 yolks are more satisfactory. The egg yolks should be put into a small basin or bowl which must be first rinsed with hot water, dried thoroughly and then set on a damp, folded dish cloth to prevent it from skidding about as you work. There is nothing worse than trying to make mayonnaise in a bowl that is sliding about all over the place like a frisky eel! To the egg yolks should be added half the acid, (this alleviates curdling to a certain extent) together with the seasonings, and then the mixture should be thoroughly beaten before the oil is added.

Now comes the tricky part which takes the time and the patience — adding the oil. It has to be done literally drop by drop until the mayonnaise is thick, glossy and holding together. Go any faster and your mayonnaise will break and stubbornly refuse to thicken. This calls for a two-hand operation and a fair amount of dexterity; one hand adding the oil and the other hand beating all the time. The oil can be added from the tip of a teaspoon (pouring it is dangerous) or from an eye dropper or from the bottle itself, provided it has been fitted with a cork from which a tiny wedge has first been removed. Personally I favour the first two methods; holding a bottle of oil for any length of time is tiring. The beating can be done with a fork, wooden spoon, a wire whisk or a portable electric hand mixer. It all depends on what you find the most comfortable. When half the oil has been beaten in and you can see for yourself that the mayonnaise is thick and glossy, the remaining oil can be added in a slow trickle while you continue to beat steadily all the time.

One evening some years ago, I was demonstrating the technique of mayonnaise making to a group of ladies who were taking a course in advanced cookery. I was gaily chatting away and beating furiously and suddenly looked down at my mayonnaise. I couldn't believe my eyes! Before these highly critical and very able ladies it had curdled on me — the first time ever! There was nothing whatever I could do to cover up the disaster, so I owned up and started the only remedial treatment I knew. They were highly amused, and at the same time most sympathetic at this unexpected turn of events, and my sudden sauce-saving operation — which worked — pleased and interested them enormously and proved a far greater success than my perfect mayonnaise could ever have done! Which all goes to prove that if a mayonnaise does curdle, it isn't the end of the world, provided you know what to do to put it right!

Break a fresh egg into a clean basin. (If it has come straight from the refrigerator, stand it in a bowl of warm water for a few minutes to warm up.) Gradually beat the curdled mayonnaise into it, a drop at a time. As it starts to thicken, add the mayonnaise a little more quickly, but not too quickly or you will end up with a curdled sauce yet again!

Mayonnaise is allergic to stormy weather and should not be made when a storm threatens or when there is one raging above. It just won't work.

The sauce will keep for approximately ten days in a cool place. Transfer it to a plastic container with an air-tight lid and put it into the larder or the least cold part of the refrigerator. Avoid chilling the mayonnaise as it will separate. If you have no air-tight plastic container, put the mayonnaise into a basin and cover it closely with aluminium foil.

Mayonnaise sauce and its variations are in complete rapport with most cold cooked foods and salads, whether combined with them to produce specific dishes or used as a dressing. It is one of the most adaptable and versatile sauces of all and its uses are endless — hence its world-wide popularity.

66 CLASSIC MAYONNAISE SAUCE

Cooking time nil   *Serves* 6—8

2 egg yolks (use large eggs)
$\frac{1}{2}$ level teaspoon salt
$\frac{1}{2}$ level teaspoon dry or Continental mustard
$\frac{1}{4}$ level teaspoon castor sugar
shake of cayenne pepper
3 dessertspoons fresh lemon juice, strained
$\frac{1}{2}$ pint oil (olive, groundnut or corn, or mixture according to taste)
1 dessertspoon wine vinegar (optional)
1 or 2 dessertspoons boiling water

Put the egg yolks into a warm bowl. Add salt, mustard, sugar, cayenne pepper and 1 dessertspoon lemon juice. Beat thoroughly. Add half the oil, drop by drop, beating continuously all the time. When the mayonnaise is as thick as stiffly whipped cream, add another dessertspoon of lemon juice. Still beating all the time, add rest of oil in a thin, steady stream. Stir in rest of lemon juice (and vinegar if used) then lastly fold in the boiling water.

If the mayonnaise is too thick for your personal taste and requirements, thin it down by adding an extra dessertspoon of boiling water, cream or lemon juice.

67 BLENDER MAYONNAISE

This must be the cook's joy! Easy and quick to make and entirely trouble-free and reliable. I can't fault mayonnaise made in the blender at all, although it does have (due to the inclusion of egg white) a lighter, frothy texture than mayonnaise made by hand.

Cooking time nil

Serves 6—8

1 large egg
½ level teaspoon dry or Continental mustard
½ level teaspoon salt
a shake of white pepper
½ level teaspoon granulated or castor sugar
½ pint oil (olive, groundnut or corn or mixture)
3 dessertspoons fresh lemon juice, strained
1 dessertspoon wine vinegar (optional)
2 dessertspoons boiling water

Put the egg, mustard, salt, pepper, sugar and 4 tablespoons of the oil into the blender. Cover and blend until smooth. Uncover and with blender at medium speed, slowly add ¼ pint oil and all the lemon juice. Blend until smooth and creamy. Slowly add rest of oil (and vinegar if used) and continue to blend until the mayonnaise is thick. Transfer to bowl and stir in the boiling water. If mayonnaise is too thick, thin it down by adding another dessertspoon boiling water, thin cream or lemon juice.

68 AVOCADO MAYONNAISE

It's rich and expensive and luxurious and the ultimate in smoothness and should be tried once in a lifetime at least! I was introduced to this sauce fairly recently and fell in love with its delicate colour and gentle flavour. It looks and tastes superb with cold chicken, hard-boiled eggs and poached salmon and is equally delicious as a dressing for mixed salads of all kinds.

It does, however, have to be made in a blender; in no other way can one obtain the smoothness which gives this mayonnaise its distinctive character.

Cooking time nil   *Serves* 4

1 large ripe avocado
4 tablespoons oil (olive, groundnut or corn, or mixture according to taste)
1 large egg
juice of 1 medium lemon
$\frac{1}{2}$ level teaspoon salt

$\frac{1}{4}$ level teaspoon castor sugar
a shake of white pepper
$\frac{1}{2}$ level teaspoon made mustard (English for preference)
1 or 2 tablespoons single cream

Peel the avocado then cut flesh into cubes. Put into blender with oil, egg, lemon juice, salt, sugar, pepper and mustard. Blend for 10—15 seconds or until thick and creamy. Transfer to a bowl and, if liked, thin down with cream. Use straight away or cover closely and refrigerate.

69 NO-EGG MAYONNAISE

For those who find the egg and oil combination of home-made mayonnaise too rich, here's a no-egg version, also made in the blender, which is light and fluffy, but at the same time thick and creamy looking and extremely well flavoured. Because it's on the pallid side, I would suggest colouring it with a few drops of yellow food colouring.

Cooking time nil   *Serves* 4—6

6 tablespoons corn oil
1 oz. instant non-fat milk granules
4 tablespoons hot water
$\frac{1}{2}$ level teaspoon salt

$\frac{1}{2}$ level teaspoon dry mustard
a shake of white pepper
3 dessertspoons wine or cider vinegar
yellow food colouring

Put oil, milk granules and water into the blender. Blend at low speed until well mixed. With blender still set to low, add salt, mustard, pepper and the vinegar. Cover and blend at high speed for 30—40 seconds, until the mayonnaise is thick and smooth. Transfer to a bowl and tint pale yellow with food colouring. Use straight away, or cover tightly and refrigerate.

70 AÏOLI SAUCE OR GARLIC MAYONNAISE

This is potent, but idolised by garlic lovers! If you are one of them you will relish this sauce over cold boiled potatoes, cooked beetroot, freshwater fish, salt cod, boiled beetroot, tomato salad and boiled beef. There are three versions. The first is a Spanish one which is immensely popular with meat, fish and rabbit, and which uses an astronomical amount of garlic to oil, something like 15 cloves of garlic to a pint. I shall dismiss this one because I can't imagine anyone outside Spain being able to cope with life and people after partaking of this heady sauce!

The second is Classic Mayonnaise Sauce to which 1 or 2 cloves of finely chopped garlic have been added. (Sometimes the garlic is cooked first in water until soft and then chopped. It makes the whole thing much more subtle.) The third version has a recipe all to itself which is:

Cooking time nil   *Serves* 4—6

½ large slice white bread   large pinch of salt
warm milk   ½ pint olive oil (olive and no
4 garlic cloves, very finely   other here)
   chopped   2 teaspoons cold water
2 egg yolks   juice of ½ a lemon

Soak the bread in the milk then squeeze dry. Put into a bowl and, using a wooden spoon, beat to a smooth cream with garlic and egg yolks. Season with salt. Add half the oil, drop by drop, beating continuously all the time. As soon as the sauce has thickened and is the same consistency as mayonnaise, add rest of oil in a thin, steady stream, still beating vigorously all the time. Stir in the water and lemon juice and the mayonnaise is now ready to serve.

Should it separate, treat it in exactly the same way as you would treat a curdled mayonnaise (page 62).

71 SKORDALIA

A variation of Aïoli sauce — breadcrumb version — is Skordalia from Greece.

Make up the sauce (see Recipe 70) then stir in 1 or 2 oz. ground almonds, 1 oz. extra breadcrumbs, 1 extra dessertspoon lemon juice and 1 level tablespoon chopped parsley.

72 ANDALOUSE SAUCE

Pleasantly flavoured with tomato purée (or tomato paste) and pimento (the sweet red pepper obtainable in jars or cans), this sauce goes very well with hard-boiled eggs, cold poultry and cold roast veal.

Make up recipe for Classic Mayonnaise Sauce, Blender Mayonnaise or No-Egg Mayonnaise (see Recipes 66, 67 and 69). Thoroughly stir in 2 level tablespoons tomato purée (or paste) and 2 level tablespoons finely chopped pimento. Season to taste.

73 CABOUL SAUCE

This is mayonnaise mildly seasoned with curry powder. Try it with cold poultry, pork or hard-boiled eggs.

Make up recipe for Classic Mayonnaise Sauce,
Blender Mayonnaise or No-Egg Mayonnaise (see
Recipes 66, 67 and 69). Stir in 2—4 level teaspoons
curry powder according to taste.

74 CHANTILLY MAYONNAISE

A sumptuous, glamorous combination of mayonnaise
and whipped cream. It is very rich but mild in
flavour and is delicious with cold poultry, hard-boiled
eggs, cold asparagus, in avocado pears and with any
cold fish. In America, it is served with fruit salad!

Make up recipe for Classic Mayonnaise Sauce or
Blender Mayonnaise (see Recipes 66 and 67). Stir in
$\frac{1}{4}$ pint (or half this amount if preferred) of softly
whipped cream. Season to taste before serving.

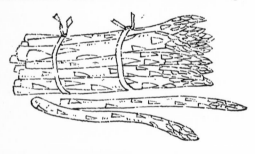

75 COCKTAIL SAUCE

A rosy pink sauce, very good for any seafood cocktail,
such as prawn, lobster or crab. It also enlivens canned
salmon and tuna fish and hard-boiled eggs.

Make up recipe for Classic Mayonnaise, Blender
Mayonnaise or No-Egg Mayonnaise (see Recipes 66,
67 and 69). Stir in 2 level tablespoons tomato purée
(or paste), 2 level teaspoons horseradish sauce, 1
teaspoon Worcestershire sauce and a shake of Tabasco.

76 EPICURIENNE SAUCE

A piquant mayonnaise, very pleasant with cold meats
of all kinds, hard-boiled eggs and cold boiled potatoes.
Although gherkins are recommended in the recipe,
a double quantity of chopped dill pickle may be used.

Make up recipe for Classic Mayonnaise, Blender
Mayonnaise or No-Egg Mayonnaise (see Recipes 66,
67 and 69). Stir in 2 level tablespoons chopped gherkin
(or double that amount of dill pickle) and 2 level
tablespoons sweet pickle.

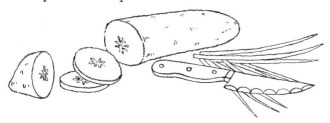

77 CUCUMBER SAUCE

A sadly neglected sauce, which is a great pity because
nothing tastes quite as good with cold salmon, salmon
trout and other cold fish dishes. It is a fresh-tasting
and delicate mayonnaise and deserves to be made more
often than it is.

Make up recipe for Classic Mayonnaise, Blender
Mayonnaise or No-Egg Mayonnaise (see Recipes 66,
67 and 69). Stir in quarter of a peeled cucumber
(coarsely grated and very well drained), 2 level
teaspoons snipped chives and 2 level teaspoons parsley.

78 GREEN MAYONNAISE (SAUCE VERTE)

A full-flavoured mayonnaise containing a wide selection of herbs and green vegetables. To give this sauce
its characteristic flavour and colour, the herbs should

be fresh whenever possible. It goes perfectly with all cold fish dishes, particularly with salmon.

Make up recipe for Classic Mayonnaise, Blender Mayonnaise or No-Egg Mayonnaise (see Recipes 66, 67 and 69). Coarsely chop 3 level dessertspoons parsley, 3 level dessertspoons tarragon or chervil, 3 level dessertspoons chives, 2 oz. spinach or 1 oz. watercress. Put into a bowl and cover with boiling water. Drain thoroughly and chop very finely. Stir into mayonnaise.

79 GUAYMAS SAUCE

This is a pale orange-coloured mayonnaise, deliciously flavoured with tomato sauce and stuffed olives. Ideally, the tomato sauce used should be home-made. If this is not possible, use instead a $\frac{1}{4}$ pint thick tomato purée made from a small can of Italian peeled tomatoes. If time permits, simmer the purée slowly for 15 minutes with $\frac{1}{2}$ a teaspoon of sugar, a pinch of basil, a teaspoon of butter and salt and pepper to taste. Leave it to get completely cold before using. Try the mayonnaise with any cold meat, over hard-boiled eggs and portions of cold poultry, with shellfish, in a potato salad, in halved avocados or over chilled artichoke hearts.

Make up any one of the recipes given for Mayonnaise. Stir in $\frac{1}{4}$ pint thick tomato purée and 1 or 2 level tablespoons finely chopped pimento-stuffed green olives.

80 LOUIS SAUCE

This is a classic mayonnaise with American overtones! It was created by an unknown chef called Louis early this century and a restaurant in San Francisco was one of the first places to serve it with cold crab and salad. Since then both the dish, Crab Louis, and the sauce have won recognition and a fair amount of fame and the sauce is now used not only with crab, but also with lobster, prawns and green salads. It is rich and creamy-tasting, due to the addition of softly whipped cream. Make up recipe for Classic Mayonnaise, Blender Mayonnaise or No-Egg Mayonnaise (see Recipes 66, 67 and 69). Stir in 2—3 tablespoons chilli sauce (this depends on taste, you can add more if you like, or less if your palate can't stand too much heat!), 3—4 tablespoons softly whipped cream, ½ a small finely chopped green pepper (de-seeded first), 1 level tablespoon finely chopped spring onion (use green parts as well) and 2 dessertspoons lemon juice.

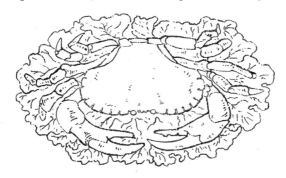

81 MAXIMILIAN SAUCE

This is basically the well-known Tartare Sauce with the addition of tomato purée. It, too, should be reserved exclusively for all fried fish dishes.

Make up recipe for Classic Mayonnaise, Blender Mayonnaise or No-Egg Mayonnaise (see Recipes 66, 67 and 69). Stir in 1 level tablespoon tomato purée, 2—3 tablespoons finely chopped gherkins, 3 level dessertspoons finely chopped capers and 1 level tablespoon very finely chopped parsley. If the sauce is very thick, thin it with a little dry white wine.

82 MOUSQUETAIRE (OR MUSKETEER) SAUCE

This sauce, well-flavoured with onions and white wine, is particularly good with cold meats of all descriptions.

Make up recipe for Classic Mayonnaise, Blender Mayonnaise or No-Egg Mayonnaise (see Recipes 66, 67 and 69). Finely chop either 1 level tablespoon shallot, the white part of a spring onion or Spanish onion. Put it into a saucepan with 2 tablespoons dry white wine. Simmer it until no wine remains. Allow to cool then add the shallot or onion to the mayonnaise.

83 RÉMOULADE SAUCE

Another cold sauce with a variety of herbs and the subtle flavour of anchovy. Many books recommend using anchovy essence, but I find canned anchovies (in oil) preferable. Mustard is also included and you can take your choice between French, which should be used, or English which can be used, again it's a matter of taste. The sauce goes well with shellfish, hard-boiled eggs, cold meat and cold poultry.

Make up recipe for Classic Mayonnaise, Blender Mayonnaise or No-Egg Mayonnaise (see Recipes 66, 67 and 69). Stir in 3—4 anchovy fillets (depending on your taste), 1 level teaspoon French or made English mustard, 1 teaspoon each, finely chopped parsley, tarragon and chervil (fresh if possible), 1 dessertspoon chopped gherkins and 1 dessertspoon chopped capers.

84 RUSSIAN SAUCE

This can be a very simple combination of mayonnaise and grated horseradish. Or it can be a luxurious concoction if caviare is added as well. (The Danish lump fish roe makes an economical substitute and it is hard to tell the difference). Sometimes tomato ketchup is used to give the sauce a pinky blush, and also onion to heighten the flavour. I, myself, stir in 2 or 3 tablespoons of whipped cream at the end. I know it is extravagant but it rounds the mayonnaise off to perfection. Serve it with shellfish, eggs and cold poultry. It is also good spooned over mixed salads.

Make up recipe for Classic Mayonnaise, Blender Mayonnaise or No-Egg Mayonnaise (see Recipes 66, 67 and 69). Stir in 1 level tablespoon finely grated horseradish. If liked, add 2—3 tablespoons caviare or lump fish roe and/or 2—3 tablespoons tomato ketchup and 1—2 teaspoons finely grated onion with cream.

85 SWEDISH SAUCE

This is an interesting sauce made with mayonnaise and thick apple sauce or purée plus the addition of a small amount of grated horseradish. It blends well with cold roast pork, smoked meats and sliced sausages.

Make up recipe for Classic Mayonnaise, Blender Mayonnaise or No-Egg Mayonnaise (see Recipes 66, 67 and 69). Stir in an equal amount of thick, un-sweetened (or sweetened if you prefer) apple sauce or purée and 1 or 2 level teaspoons grated horseradish.

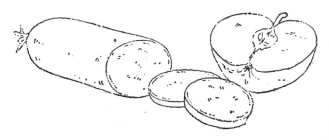

86 TARTARE SAUCE

The classic sauce for fried fish.

Make up recipe for Classic Mayonnaise, Blender Mayonnaise or No-Egg Mayonnaise (see Recipes 66, 67 and 69). Stir in 2—3 level tablespoons finely chopped gherkins, 3 level dessertspoons finely chopped capers and 1 level tablespoon very finely chopped parsley.

87 THOUSAND ISLAND SAUCE

American, like the Louis sauce. It is a hearty mayonnaise with colourful and appetising additions and can be served with eggs, shellfish and over wedges of crisp lettuce. Try it on cold poultry — it's good!

Make up recipe for Classic Mayonnaise, Blender Mayonnaise or No-Egg Mayonnaise (see Recipes 66, 67 and 69). Stir in 1 or 2 finely chopped hard-boiled eggs, 1 or 2 tablespoons chilli sauce (or 2—3 tablespoons tomato ketchup if a milder flavour is preferred), 2 level tablespoons finely chopped stuffed olives, 1 level tablespoon finely chopped onion or snipped chives and 1 level tablespoon finely chopped parsley. Whipped cream (about 1—3 tablespoons) stirred in at the end is an optional extra.

88 WATERCRESS SAUCE

A beautifully flavoured and sophisticated sauce and the height of simplicity. Serve it with all cold fish dishes.

Make up recipe for Classic Mayonnaise, Blender Mayonnaise or No-Egg Mayonnaise (see Recipes 66, 67 and 69). Stir in a quarter bunch of very finely chopped watercress.

Butter Sauces

That which is not good is not delicious
To a well-govern'd and wise appetite

These are made solely from melted butter with one or two additions. The sauces, which are exquisitely flavoured and rich, are simple in the extreme and can be made in a matter of minutes.

A gentleman by the name of G. Read, author of an 18th century book called 'The Cook', gives advice on saucepans for Butter Sauces and refers also to comments from Dr. Kitchener who was, at that time, 'an able physician and the most learned and scientific writer upon the culinary arts'. This is what he said: 'You should take care that your saucepan for melted butter be always well-tinned and kept delicately clean. Some recommend a silver saucepan, but this seems to us to be a stupid piece of extravagance'. Dr. Kitchener, however, who talks a great deal about economy, gravely tells us that a pint silver saucepan will not cost more than four or five pounds!

The culinary arts obviously held rich rewards for

Dr. Kitchener. These days we are a little more liberal in our thinking. Butter sauces can be made in any kind of saucepan whether it is enamel, stainless steel, glass or aluminium. What *does* matter is the way the butter is treated before the sauce is made. It has to be clarified first. All butter contains milky solids and unless these are removed, the sauces will look curdled, bitty, cloudy and unpleasant.

Clarifying butter is a fairly simple operation and methods for doing it haven't changed much in the last hundred years. Mrs. Beeton did it this way: 'Put the butter in a basin before the fire, and when it melts, stir it round once or twice and let it settle. Do not strain it unless absolutely necessary, as it causes too much waste. Pour it gently off into a clean, dry jar, carefully leaving all sediment behind. Let it cool and carefully exclude air by means of a bladder, or a piece of wash leather, tied over. If the butter is salty, it may be washed before melting, when it is to be used for sweet dishes.' Our friend, Mr. G. Read, used much the same technique but he strained his butter; presumably he wasn't as worried about economy as Mrs. Beeton! 'Put the butter in a clean saucepan over a clear, slow fire, and when it is melted, carefully skim off the froth, which will swim on the top; let it stand for a minute or two for the impurities to sink to the bottom then pour the clear butter through a sieve into a basin, leaving the sediment at the bottom of the pan.'

You can try either of the above two methods or this one which is a modern adaptation. Put the butter into a saucepan and melt over a very low heat. Leave to stand 5 minutes. Gently pour off the butter, leaving the sediment behind in the saucepan, or strain it through fine muslin into a clean basin. The butter should be crystal clear — rather like melted honey.

89 BROWN BUTTER SAUCE

For hot asparagus, broccoli and brains. It is also extremely good with hot celery hearts and poached heads of chicory.

Cooking time 3—5 minutes   *Serves* 4

3 oz. clarified butter

Put the butter into a small saucepan or frying pan. Stand over a low heat and leave until butter turns light brown. Remove from heat and serve.

90 BLACK BUTTER SAUCE (OR BEURRE NOISETTE)

This sauce is not really black but dark brown with a slight nutty flavour and fragrant aroma. It is sharpened with a little vinegar and is perfect over poached or steamed white fish dishes, over poached eggs and over vegetables.

Cooking time 4—6 minutes   *Serves* 4

3 oz. clarified butter   1 teaspoon vinegar

Put the butter into a small saucepan or frying pan. Stand over a low heat and leave until butter turns dark brown. Remove from heat and stir in vinegar.

91 MEUNIÈRE (OR LEMON) BUTTER SAUCE

This is much the same as Brown Butter Sauce except that lemon juice, parsley and a light shake of pepper are added as well. It has a hint of sharpness — pleasant with poached and steamed fish dishes and with boiled chicken. Although no book recommends adding lemon peel, I do because it greatly improves the flavour and adds a subtle hint of freshness which a rich sauce like this needs.

Cooking time 3—5 minutes   *Serves* 4

3 oz. clarified butter
1 level tablespoon finely chopped parsley
2 teaspoons lemon juice

$\frac{1}{4}$ level teaspoon finely grated lemon peel
white pepper

Put the butter into a small saucepan or frying pan. Stand over a low heat and leave until butter turns a light brown. Remove from heat. Add parsley, lemon juice and peel and season to taste with pepper.

92 BLACK BUTTER SAUCE WITH CAPERS

This is a more piquant sauce containing chopped capers and a little vinegar. It is appetising with poached skate and other white fish dishes and also with brains.

Cooking time 4—6 minutes   *Serves* 4

3 oz. clarified butter
1 level teaspoon vinegar

2 level dessertspoons chopped capers

Put the butter into a small saucepan or frying pan. Stand over a low heat and leave until butter turns a dark brown. Remove from heat and stir in vinegar and capers. Serve straight away.

93 BUTTER CRUMB SAUCE

A rather special sauce for vegetables, especially cauliflower, boiled onions, leeks and carrots.

Cooking time 5—6 minutes   *Serves* 4

3 oz. clarified butter
1 dessertspoon very finely chopped onion
2 level tablespoons dried white breadcrumbs
1 hard-boiled egg, finely chopped
2 teaspoons lemon juice
2 level teaspoons finely chopped parsley

Put the butter into a small saucepan and stand over a low heat. When butter is hot, add the onion and fry gently until it is soft but not brown. Add breadcrumbs and continue to cook, stirring all the time, until they turn biscuit coloured. Remove from heat and stir in egg, lemon juice and parsley. Serve straight away.

94 ALMOND BUTTER SAUCE

This is in the unconventional category and not a truly classic sauce as the butter ones are. Nevertheless, it is too beautiful to be kept only as a garnish (which is what it is considered to be) so I am adding it as a sauce for good measure! It goes splendidly with any poached or grilled fish, with fried or grilled trout, poached or boiled chicken and with vegetables such as marrow, cauliflower and sprouts.

Cooking time approximately *Serves* 4
5—6 minutes

3 oz. whole almonds   3 teaspoons lemon juice
3 oz. clarified butter

Drop the almonds into boiling water. Leave for 5 minutes then drain. Slide off almond skins and discard. Dry nuts thoroughly in a clean tea-towel then cut into thin strips or slivers. Put butter into a small saucepan or frying pan. Add the almonds and leave over a low heat until both the butter and the nuts turn a light brown. Remove from heat and stir in lemon juice. Serve straight away.

As these Butter sauces are unthickened, any solid additions, such as parsley, capers and the like, will drop to the bottom. It is unavoidable but there are two ways round this. Either spoon the sauce over the food before you serve it (which is fine if you are one big happy family and you know everybody's taste), or pour the sauce into a sauce-boat and put it on the table with a ladle so that people are able to stir the sauce, and thus distribute the additions, before helping themselves.

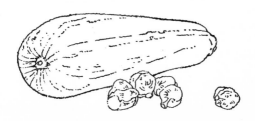

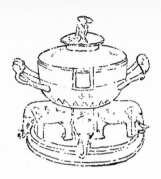

Beurres Composés

Some people have a foolish way of not minding, or pretending not to mind, what they eat; for my part, I mind my belly very studiously and very carefully, and I look upon it that he who does not mind his belly, will hardly mind anything else.

Beurres composés — or savoury butters — start off as solid sauces which quickly melt over hot food and becomes liquid sauces, rather like uncooked versions of the Butter sauces in the previous section. They are made by creaming butter, and here again I would recommend unsalted or only very slightly salted butter, with an assortment of different ingredients which will vary according to the dishes with which the butters are to be served. They are not in the least bit elaborate or difficult to prepare and they do make elegant and decorative garnishes, especially if the butters are first chilled and cut into shapes or curls.

Many classic cookery books recommend passing the Savoury Butters through a fine sieve. I don't do this because it is too time consuming and not altogether necessary, especially if the additions have been very finely chopped in the first place. To make these composition butters successfully, the butter must be soft and beaten with a wooden spoon until it's the consistency and colour of rich whipped cream. After the additions have been stirred or beaten in, the butter should be put on to a piece of aluminium foil or waxed paper and either shaped into a block for butter balls and curls, into a $\frac{1}{4}$-inch thick square or oblong for fancy shapes, or into a long roll, the diameter of a penny, for pats. It should then be lightly wrapped and well chilled so that it becomes firm and easy later to mould, curl or cut.

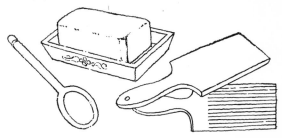

To make butter balls, you can use the old-fashioned serrated wooden butter hands that look like squashed-up cricket bats. Dip them in hot water and lightly roll hazelnut-sized pieces of the flavoured butter in between the two hands until they form balls. The art here is to hold the underneath butter hand still and firm and rotate the top one. Alternatively, you can use a melon baller; one of those kitchen gadgets with a wooden handle in the middle and a hollow scoop at either end, one slightly larger than the other. Dip one of the ends in hot water, scoop out the butter ball and drop it into a bowl of iced water. Repeat this until you have as many balls as you need. Curls are quite easy too. Dip the butter curler in hot water and draw it lightly across the surface of the butter. You should get a serrated curl. If not, try again because it does take a bit of practice. When once you've mastered the technique, drop the curls into iced water or stand them on a mound of ice cubes.

Fancy shapes can be made with small assorted biscuit cutters dipped in hot water, or a knife, also dipped in hot water. Or pats can simply be sliced off the butter roll, whatever thickness is preferred. If one cares to take the time and trouble, each little shape or pat of butter can have, pressed on to it, a flower, spray of flowers or abstract design cut from fresh herbs, pieces of red pimento or green or black olives. The butter or butters can then be dropped into iced water and left in the refrigerator until needed.

If you have a domestic deep freeze, you can make up the butters in quantity and freeze them for 4—6 weeks. Otherwise keep the butters in the refrigerator up to 24 hours, but no longer or the flavour of those containing herbs will be spoiled.

95 ANCHOVY BUTTER

A full-flavoured butter for grilled fish and beef steaks.

Serves 4

2 oz. butter
4 anchovy fillets, well-
   drained

$\frac{1}{2}$ teaspoon lemon juice

Beat the butter to a light cream. Chop the anchovies as finely as possible and beat into the butter with the lemon juice. Chill, shape and serve.

96 AMANDINE BUTTER

A delicately flavoured butter which is delicious with grilled chicken and grilled fish such as trout.

Serves 4

2 oz. butter   1 or 2 teaspoons cold water
1 oz. ground almonds

Beat the butter to a light cream. Mix almonds to a thick paste with cold water. Gradually beat into butter. Chill, shape and serve.

97 BERCY BUTTER

A fine-flavoured butter for all grilled meats, especially steaks and lamb chops.

Serves 4

2 shallots or ½ a small onion   2 level teaspoons finely chop-
2 tablespoons dry white wine   ped parsley
2 oz. butter

Finely grate shallots or onion. Put into a saucepan with the wine and simmer until only 1 teaspoon of liquid remains. Cool. Beat butter to a light cream. Gradually beat in shallots or onions and remaining wine. Lastly stir in parsley. Chill, shape and serve.

98 CAVIARE BUTTER

This gives a luxurious touch to all grilled fish dishes.

Serves 4

2 oz. butter   1 teaspoon lemon juice
1 oz. caviare (or Danish
   lump fish roe)

Beat the butter to a light cream. Pound the caviare or lump fish roe until it is as smooth as possible. Beat into butter with the lemon juice. Chill, shape and serve.

99 CHIVE BUTTER

Mildly onion flavoured, this butter goes well with grilled fish of all types, grilled meats and chicken.

Serves 4

2 oz. butter
1 level dessertspoon very finely chopped chives

1 teaspoon lemon juice or wine vinegar

Beat the butter to a light cream. Beat in chives and lemon juice or vinegar. Chill, shape and serve.

100 COLBERT BUTTER

Named after Monsieur Colbert who was a Prime Minister of Louis XIV. It is butter flavoured with parsley, lemon juice and meat extract; very good with grilled fish, grilled steaks and thick, underdone slices of hot roast beef.

Serves 4

2 oz. butter
1 level teaspoon finely chopped parsley
1 teaspoon lemon juice

large pinch of finely chopped fresh or small pinch of dried tarragon
$\frac{1}{4}$ level teaspoon meat extract

Beat the butter to a light cream. Gradually beat in all remaining ingredients. Chill, shape and serve.

101 CURRY BUTTER

Especially recommended for grilled chicken, all grilled meats and shellfish.

Serves 4

2 oz. butter
2 teaspoons curry powder
pinch of cayenne pepper

$\frac{1}{4}$ level teaspoon powdered ginger
2 teaspoons lemon juice

Beat the butter to a light cream. Stir in curry powder, cayenne pepper and ginger. Beat in lemon juice, then chill, shape and serve.

102 DEVIL BUTTER

This is somewhat on the fiery side but well worth trying with shellfish, grilled gammon steaks, grilled chops, hot boiled bacon and grilled kidneys.

Serves 4

2 oz. butter
1 level teaspoon French mustard
1 teaspoon Worcestershire sauce

a shake of Tabasco sauce or large pinch of cayenne pepper
1 teaspoon wine vinegar

Beat the butter to a light cream. Beat in the mustard, Worcestershire sauce and Tabasco sauce or cayenne pepper. Stir in vinegar, then chill, shape and serve.

103 GARLIC BUTTER

A good, strong-tasting sauce that garlic lovers will want to put on everything! Do so by all means, but remember it's supposed to be for grilled steak only and *not* for anything with a delicate flavour.

Serves 4

2—4 garlic cloves   1 teaspoon lemon juice
2 oz. butter

Cook garlic cloves in a little water for 7 minutes. Drain and chop very finely. Beat butter to a light cream then beat in garlic and lemon juice. Chill, shape and serve.

104 GREEN BUTTER

Exclusively for fish, best made with fresh herbs.

Serves 4

6 leaves of watercress   3 spinach leaves
1 level teaspoon fresh tar-   2 oz. butter
   ragon   2 level teaspoons very finely
1 level teaspoon fresh parsley   grated onion

Put watercress, tarragon, parsley and spinach into a saucepan. Cover with boiling water and leave for 4 minutes. Drain. Plunge into cold water and leave 1 minute. Drain and dry in a tea-towel. Chop very finely. Beat the butter to a light cream. Gradually beat in the chopped greenery and onion. Chill, shape and serve.

105 HORSERADISH BUTTER

For grilled steaks, grilled herrings and grilled mackerel.

Serves 4

2 oz. butter
1—2 level teaspoons very
  finely grated horseradish

1 teaspoon lemon juice

Beat the butter to a light cream. Beat in horseradish and lemon juice. Chill, shape and serve.

106 MAÎTRE D'HÔTEL BUTTER

Another one for fish.

Serves 4

2 oz. butter
1 level teaspoon finely chopped parsley

2 teaspoons lemon juice

Beat the butter to a light cream. Beat in parsley and lemon juice. Chill, shape and serve.

107 MUSTARD BUTTER

Delicious with grilled gammon, grilled steaks, pork and lamb chops, shellfish, grilled salmon, grilled mackerel and grilled herrings.

Serves 4

2 oz. butter
1 level teaspoon made English or French mustard

1 teaspoon lemon juice

Beat the butter to a light cream. Beat in mustard and lemon juice. Chill, shape and serve.

108 PAPRIKA BUTTER

Sometimes called Hungarian butter. Try it with grilled veal chops, hot ham, grilled gammon and shellfish.

Serves 4

2 oz. butter
1 level teaspoon paprika

1 level teaspoon very finely grated onion
1 teaspoon wine vinegar

Beat the butter to a light cream. Beat in paprika, onion and vinegar. Chill, shape and serve.

109 PRAWN (OR SHRIMP) BUTTER

Again for fish.

Serves 4

2 oz. butter
1 oz. peeled prawns

pinch of cayenne pepper
1 teaspoon lemon juice

Beat the butter to a light cream. Very finely chop the prawns. Beat into butter with cayenne pepper and lemon juice. Chill, shape and serve.

110 SMOKED SALMON BUTTER

The height of luxury because it gives a regal touch to the simplest of foods. See what it does to grilled cod!

Serves 4

2 oz. butter
1 oz. of the best smoked salmon

1 teaspoon lemon juice
light shake of pepper

Beat the butter to a light cream. Chop the salmon very finely. Beat into butter with lemon juice and pepper. Chill, shape and serve.

Barbecue Sauces

Oldfield, with more than happy throat evoked,
Cries, Send me, gods, a whole hog barbecued.

The barbecuing of foods, which goes back to the Old
Testament, is associated with outdoor eating and
the word barbecue originally meant to truss and roast,
over direct heat, a whole animal, from the French
barbe à queue (from beard to tail). It is a very popular
and well-loved method of cooking meat and poultry
in North America, but in Britain this style of alfresco
eating, which requires special cooking equipment if
it's to be done properly, has never caught on to the
same extent. Some people do make brief attempts,
when the climate permits, to cook foods over a brazier
or barbecue pit, but the nearest the majority get to the
original conception of a barbecue is when they light
the bonfire on Guy Fawkes' night and cook chestnuts
and jacket potatoes in the peripheral flames!

This does not mean, fortunately, that we can't make
full use of Barbecue sauces. We grill foods and we spit
roast them in rotisseries and for this type of cooking,
the sauces are ideal. They lend piquancy and character

to any piece of offal, meat and poultry and vastly improve their flavour. Below are a selection of mild and not so mild sauces which are suitable for meat and vegetable kebabs, chops, steaks, portions of chicken and whole birds. Because many of the sauces contain spices and because long cooking under or over fierce heat makes the spices bitter, Barbecue sauces should be spread on to foods towards the end of cooking; about two-thirds of the way through.

111 BARBECUE SAUCE FOR PORK, DUCK AND GOOSE

Cooking time about 20 to 25 minutes

1 small onion, finely chopped

4 level tablespoons tomato purée

$\frac{1}{4}$ pint water

2 tablespoons wine or cider vinegar

1 tablespoon Worcestershire sauce

$\frac{1}{2}$ level teaspoon salt

2 level teaspoons brown sugar

$\frac{1}{4}$ level teaspoon sage

1 level teaspoon paprika

1 level teaspoon chilli powder

good shake of pepper

$\frac{1}{4}$ level teaspoon mixed spice

Put all the ingredients into a saucepan. Slowly bring to the boil, stirring all the time. Simmer gently until the sauce is reduced by one-third. Use as required.

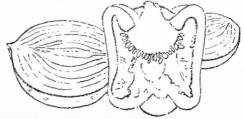

112 PICKLE BARBECUE SAUCE FOR BEEF

Cooking time about 15 to 20 minutes

2 oz. butter
1 level tablespoon finely chopped gherkins
1 tablespoon Worcestershire sauce
1 small onion, finely chopped
½ teaspoon Tabasco

juice of 1 medium lemon
2 level teaspoons brown sugar
1 small green pepper, very finely chopped
¼ level teaspoon mixed herbs
¼ pint dry red wine

Put all the ingredients into a saucepan. Slowly bring to the boil, stirring all the time. Simmer gently until the sauce is reduced by one-third. Use as required.

113 TOMATO BARBECUE SAUCE

For all meats and poultry and thick steaks of fish.
Cooking time about 35 minutes

½ oz. butter
1 tablespoon salad oil
1 medium onion, chopped
1 level tablespoon flour
¼ pint water
4 tablespoons vinegar
1 tablespoon Worcestershire sauce
juice of 1 lemon

¼ pint tomato ketchup
4 oz. skinned and chopped tomatoes
1 level teaspoon made mustard
2 oz. brown sugar
2 celery stalks, very finely chopped
½ level teaspoon salt

Heat butter and oil in a saucepan. Add onion and fry gently until soft and just beginning to turn golden. Stir in flour; cook for 1 minute, stirring continuously. Gradually blend in water. Add all remaining ingredients and bring slowly to the boil, stirring all the time.

Lower heat and cover pan. Simmer gently for 30 minutes. Strain before using.

114 CIDER BARBECUE SAUCE

For fish, poultry and white meats.

Cooking time about 20 to 25 minutes

¼ pint dry cider
1 small onion, finely grated
¼ level teaspoon mixed herbs
2 tablespoons lemon juice
2 level teaspoons granulated sugar
2 tablespoons salad oil
3 tablespoons tomato ketchup
½ level teaspoon dry mustard
2 teaspoons Worcestershire sauce
1 level teaspoon paprika

Put all the ingredients into a saucepan. Slowly bring to the boil, stirring continuously. Simmer gently until the sauce is reduced by one-third. Use as required.

Classic Italian Sauces

To think of Italy in terms only of spaghetti, tomato sauce, pizza and minestrone is sad and wrong, for Italians have made a habit of good eating since Roman times when the mammoth banquets and daylong feasting and drinking made history.

The charm and popularity of this country's gastronomy lies in its basic simplicity and unpretentiousness. To every Italian cook and epicure and in every Italian household — be it humble or noble — the quality and freshness of the ingredients matter most. Less importance is attached to elaborate and formal presentation of dishes and complicated finishing touches. A bowl of piping hot pasta, glistening with pure melted butter or oil and smothered in Parmesan cheese needs no further adornment. It is good enough as it is.

The only two classic sauces used to any extent in Italy are the Béchamel and mayonnaise. Other than that the sauces are relatively simple affairs made with oil, often tomatoes and tomato purée, fresh herbs, garlic, onions, meat, game, fish and wine. The concentrated meat stocks demanded by the French sauces

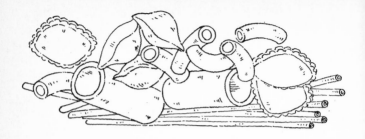

are little used. We find broth instead, made from fresh veal, beef or poultry.

Perhaps the most famous of all Italian sauces is the Bolognese; the meat and tomato sauce which in Italy is known as ragû and which is usually served with pasta in one form or another. And here I must digress from sauces for a moment and talk about the pasta itself. Outside Italy, pasta is frequently overcooked. It becomes soft, sticky and gluey and not even a good, carefully prepared sauce will do much to help it. Inside Italy, pasta is served *al dente* — soft but still firm and chewy. There are two ways of cooking pasta. One is to allow between 2 and 4 oz. per person (depending on appetite) and cook it in plenty of boiling salted water for 15—20 minutes; rarely any longer.

Another method, which I prefer, is to add the required amount of pasta to a large pan of rapidly boiling salted water. Return to boil. Remove from heat; cover it first with a folded tea-towel (the edges should just fall over the sides of the pan) and then with a saucepan lid pressed down firmly. Leave it for 20—25 minutes. In that time the pasta will cook and swell in the steam and will be perfectly *al dente*. Furthermore, you won't be troubled with sticking and boiling over. The next thing is to strain the pasta very thoroughly, put it into a warm dish and toss it with butter or the very best quality olive oil. Then you can serve it with any sauce you like, but don't let it get cold!

And now back to the Bolognese sauce which is, as its name suggests, a speciality from Bologna. It is hard to find two recipes that tally and it has more versions to its credit than almost any other Italian sauce. The best I can do is give the one I enjoy most and which seems to resemble closely those I have eaten in some parts of Italy. Serve it with lasagne verdi, spaghetti, macaroni or any other pasta to taste.

115 BOLOGNESE SAUCE

Cooking time 1¼ hours   *Serves* 4

½ oz. butter
1 dessertspoon salad oil
1 medium onion, very finely chopped
3 oz. unsmoked bacon, finely chopped
1 medium carrot, grated
1 small celery stalk, finely chopped
8 oz. raw minced beef
2 level tablespoons tomato purée

2 level teaspoons brown sugar
1 strip of lemon peel (about 3 inches long)
a large pinch of nutmeg
½ pint beef stock or water
1 wine glass of dry white wine
salt and pepper to taste
4 tablespoons single or double cream (optional)

Heat the butter and oil in a saucepan. Add the onion, bacon, carrot and celery and fry very gently until deep gold. Add the beef and fry for 5 minutes, breaking it up with a fork continuously so that it browns all over. Stir in the purée and sugar then add the lemon peel, nutmeg, stock or water, wine and seasoning to taste. Bring slowly to the boil. Lower the heat and cover pan. Simmer gently for one hour, stirring occasionally. Remove from heat and stir in the cream if used. Add to well-drained pasta and toss thoroughly.

116 MEAT SAUCE

Similar to the Bolognese sauce but with mushrooms included and slightly less tomato purée. The sauce is generally served with pasta or gnocchi.

Cooking time 1¼ hours   *Serves* 4

2 dessertspoons olive or corn oil
1 large onion, finely chopped
1 garlic clove, finely chopped (optional)
1 small carrot, grated
8 oz. raw minced beef
1 level dessertspoon flour
1 level tablespoon tomato purée
½ pint beef stock
3 tablespoons dry white wine
¼ level teaspoon dried basil
½ small bay leaf
2—3 oz. mushrooms and stalks, chopped
salt and pepper to taste

Heat oil in a saucepan. Add onion, garlic (if used) and grated carrot. Fry gently until deep gold. Add the meat and fry for 5 minutes, breaking it up with a fork continuously so that it browns all over. Stir in the flour and cook a further minute. Add purée, then gradually stir in stock and wine. Add basil and bay leaf and slowly bring to the boil, stirring. Lower heat and simmer gently, uncovered, for 45 minutes. Stir frequently. Add mushrooms and salt and pepper to taste. Simmer a further 15 minutes.

117 NEAPOLITAN TOMATO SAUCE

This is a versatile sauce which can be served with meat, poultry and every kind of pasta. Although few Italian recipe books advise adding sugar to a tomato sauce, I always do because it counteracts the acidity of the tomatoes and, in my opinion, gives the sauce a much better flavour.

Cooking time 45 minutes *Serves* 4
    to 1 hour

2 lb. red tomatoes (or use 1 lb. 12 oz. can of Italian peeled tomatoes)
1 oz. butter
1 dessertspoon olive or corn oil
2 level teaspoons granulated sugar
1 small onion, finely grated
2—3 leaves of fresh basil or ½ level teaspoon dried
1 level dessertspoon finely chopped parsley
salt and pepper to taste

Skin the tomatoes and rub them through a fine sieve. If used, the canned tomatoes will, of course, already be skinned.

    Put the resultant purée into a saucepan with the butter, oil, sugar, onion, basil, parsley and salt and pepper (freshly milled black pepper is the best to use) to taste. Bring the sauce to the boil, stirring continuously. Simmer slowly, covered, for 45 minutes— 1 hour or until the sauce is very thick.

118 SALSA ALLA PIZZAIOLA

Another version of tomato sauce which also comes from Naples. It is strongly flavoured with garlic and herbs and can be served with beef, lamb, poultry, veal and all sorts of pasta dishes.

Cooking time 20 minutes   *Serves* 4

2 lb. small red tomatoes (or 1lb. 12 oz. can of Italian peeled tomatoes)
1 tablespoon olive oil
2 large garlic cloves, coarsely chopped
2 level dessertspoons coarsely chopped parsley
1 level teaspoon dried basil or oregano
½ level teaspoon salt
1 level teaspoon granulated sugar
pepper to taste

If using fresh tomatoes, skin them first then chop them up coarsely. Put into a saucepan with all remaining ingredients. Slowly bring to the boil. Lower heat and cook, uncovered, for 15—20 minutes, stirring occasionally, but taking care not to break up the tomatoes much; they should be in pieces rather than pulpy.

119 LIVER SAUCE

Usually made with chicken livers, mushrooms and onions, this is a substantial sauce to serve with gnocchi, spaghetti or noodles.

Cooking time 30—35 minutes *Serves* 4

8 oz. chicken livers
1 oz. flour
1 oz. butter
1 small onion, very finely chopped
4 oz. mushrooms and stalks, finely chopped
¼ pint chicken stock or water
6 tablespoons dry white wine
½ level teaspoon salt

Cut the liver into ½-inch cubes and coat them with flour. Melt the butter in a saucepan. Add the onion, fry gently until pale gold. Add liver and mushrooms and fry slowly for a further 5 minutes, turning with a wooden spoon all the time. Gradually blend in stock or water and wine. Add salt and bring sauce slowly to the boil, stirring continuously. Simmer, uncovered, for 15 minutes, stirring occasionally.

120 MUSHROOM SAUCE

A delicate sauce for pasta, veal, poultry and lamb. It can be made with tiny button mushrooms left whole, or larger ones cut into thin slices.

Cooking time 20—25 minutes *Serves* 4

1 oz. butter
1 dessertspoon olive oil
1 small onion, chopped
1 garlic clove, very finely chopped
2 level tablespoons finely chopped parsley
1 small celery stalk, very finely chopped
1 level tablespoon flour
12 oz. mushrooms
$\frac{1}{4}$ pint poultry or veal stock
salt and pepper to taste

Heat the butter and oil in a saucepan. Add the onion and garlic and fry gently until light gold. Add parsley and celery and cook a further minute. Stir in flour then add mushrooms and stock. Bring to the boil, stirring continuously. Lower heat and cover the pan. Simmer for 15 minutes, stirring occasionally. Season to taste and serve.

121 ANCHOVY SAUCE

A very rich and full-flavoured sauce indeed, for the stout hearted only! In Italy, it is served with whole baby lamb and also with pasta. Salted anchovies, which are to be found in Continental delicatessen, can be used, but they should be soaked in several changes of cold water for a good 12 hours to get rid of some of the salt. Safer perhaps, are canned anchovies in oil which are generally milder and more readily available. A little of this sauce goes a long way; it is meant to oil and flavour the hot food rather than add moisture.

Cooking time 10 minutes   *Serves* 4—6

2 tablespoons olive oil
1 oz. butter
1 garlic clove, finely chopped
2 oz. can anchovy fillets in oil
4 level tablespoons finely chopped parsley

½ level teaspoon dried basil or 1 teaspoon chopped fresh basil
freshly milled black pepper to taste

Heat the oil and butter in a small saucepan. Add the garlic and cook *very slowly* for 5 minutes. Meanwhile, open the can of anchovies and drain the oil into the saucepan. Chop the anchovies coarsely and add to pan with the parsley and basil. Heat through for a further 5 minutes then season to taste with pepper.

122 BAGNA CAUDA

This is practically the same as Anchovy Sauce (see Recipe 121), the only difference being the addition of 1 or 2 sliced white truffles — if you can get them. Its purpose, however, is different. It is not served as a sauce over anything or mixed with anything, but treated as a kind of pre-drink dip. It is always served hot and is accompanied with vegetables (raw or cooked) which are dipped into it. The vegetables used depend, to a certain extent, on the season but canned artichoke hearts (well-drained), 2-inch lengths of celery, pieces of red or green pepper and small pieces of cauliflower are the most acceptable.

123 PESTO

This is a cold sauce — or better still flavouring — which was, until the introduction of modern kitchen gadgets, always made in a pestle and mortar; hence its name. It is beloved by the Genoese and is, indeed, a speciality from Genoa. It is made from oil, pine nuts and / or walnuts, Pecorino cheese (or Parmesan cheese), garlic and fresh leaves of basil. The emphasis is on fresh here because dried basil won't do at all. It is used, rather as the Anchovy Sauce is used, to flavour and oil hot pasta and in some parts of Italy it is stirred into piping hot minestrone, to add to and improve its flavour. Because both pine nuts and Pecorino cheese are relatively hard to find, I have used walnuts and Parmesan cheese instead (which is quite permissible). The sauce, like any condiment, is added by the table-spoon and for this reason it is impossible to say how many the quantity below will serve. However, it keeps quite well so what you don't use on one occasion can be covered with foil and kept in the refrigerator for next time.

$1\frac{1}{2}$—2 oz. fresh basil leaves
2 garlic cloves
2 oz. walnuts
2 oz. Parmesan cheese
1 tablespoon chives
1 oz. ground almonds
$\frac{1}{4}$—$\frac{1}{2}$ level teaspoon salt
shake of pepper
4 tablespoons olive oil (the very best quality available)

Coarsely chop the basil, garlic and walnuts. Put into a mortar with the cheese, chives, almonds and salt and pepper. Pound with a pestle until the mixture turns into a soft paste. Very gradually add the oil drop by drop, stirring it briskly with the pestle all the time. As soon as the oil has been worked in, the sauce is ready.

124 GARLIC SAUCE

One type of garlic sauce eaten in Italy — served with freshwater and other types of heavy fish — is very similar to the Aïoli Sauce made with breadcrumbs and given in the Mayonnaise Section on page 66. Another is a bit more fierce and should be tackled only by those with tough and resilient digestions. It is especially designed for serving with pasta.

Cooking time 8 minutes   *Serves* 6—8

3 tablespoons olive oil
2 oz. butter
4 large garlic cloves, chopped
2 level dessertspoons finely
  chopped parsley

1 level teaspoon dried basil
$\frac{1}{4}$—$\frac{1}{2}$ level teaspoon salt
pepper to taste

Heat oil and butter in a small saucepan. Add garlic and fry very gently for 5 minutes. Add all remaining ingredients and keep over a low heat for a further 5 minutes. Toss with freshly cooked hot pasta and serve straight away.

ITALIAN MAYONNAISE

Mayonnaise in Italy is eaten as much as it is anywhere else, but the Italians don't have anything like the same number of variations from the one basic recipe as the French. They enjoy their mayonnaise as it is; simply made with egg yolks, lemon juice (sometimes white wine and crushed garlic) and the very finest olive oil and are inclined to use it thick, mild and glistening, without further additions, except for parsley and fresh basil. One or two finely chopped tablespoons of each are sometimes added to ½ pint of Basic Mayonnaise, as is finely mashed canned tuna fish — about 3 to 4 oz. Both these sauces can be served with practically everything, but the tuna mayonnaise is surprisingly delicious with poultry and veal, especially if a few finely chopped black olives are added as well.

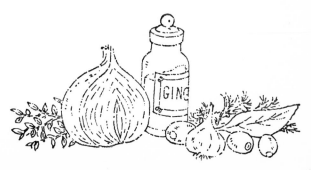

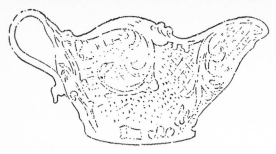

Miscellaneous Savoury Sauces

*Kent sir — everybody knows Kent —
apples, cherries, hops and women*

Although the best cooking apple, the Bramley, now
flourishes in Kent, the very first one started life in
Nottingham as long ago as 1805. Just for a bit of fun,
a little girl planted an apple pip in the garden of
a Nottingham cottage. Where the pip came from no-
body knows, but it took root and, under her loving
care, grew into a large, fruit-bearing tree. During the
next fifty years the little girl, now a grandmother, gave
away many cuttings to friends who grafted them on to
various other trees in the area. And so, more by luck
than by judgment, the first Bramleys were born. They
rapidly became popular and were considered to be
such a superb cooking apple, that a local nurseryman
asked the owner if he would allow him to distribute
the apple commercially. Permission was granted, but
on one condition: the variety had to bear the family
name of Bramley. And it does to this day.

Of course any good cooking apple can be used for Apple Sauce, traditionally served with pork dishes (I like it with pork sausages as well), roast duck and goose, but nothing gives the same mellow and fragrant flavour as the Bramley or cooks down to such a light, fluffy and snow-like purée.

125 APPLE SAUCE

Cooking time 7—10 minutes   *Serves* 4

1 lb. cooking apples
3 tablespoons water

1 level dessertspoon
  granulated sugar
$\frac{1}{4}$ oz. butter

Peel and core the apples. Slice into a saucepan and add water. Cover and cook over a low to medium heat (if the heat is too high the apples will burn and stick) until apples are well broken down and soft. Remove from heat. Beat to a pulp, then add sugar and butter. Continue beating until melted. Serve hot or cold.

126 APPLE SAUCE WITH CIDER

This can be served with the same dishes as Apple Sauce, but it is also very good with lamb and ham. This is made in exactly the same way as ordinary

Apple Sauce (see Recipe 125), but 3 tablespoons cider — which may be dry or sweet — are used instead of the water.

127 APPLE SAUCE (brown)

This comes from my early Mrs. Beeton and is a pleasing sauce with hot roast pork, boiled ham, roast duck and goose and hot smoked meats. I give below the exact recipe as it was written over a hundred years ago!

6 good-sized apples
½ pint of brown gravy
cayenne to taste

Put the gravy in a stew pan, and add the apples, after having pared, cored and quartered them. Let them simmer gently until tender, beat them to a pulp and season with cayenne.

This hundred or so year old recipe (from 'The Cook') is quaint in that is uses apple peel instead of a lid; very sensible when you think about it because so much flavour is in the skins. 'Take 4 or 5 juicy apples, 2 tablespoonfuls of cold water or cider; instead of putting a lid on, place parings over the apples, and put them by a gentle fire. When they sink down, remove the saucepan from the fire, and beat up the apples; take the parings from the top first, add a bit of butter, a teaspoonful of fine powdered sugar, and a dust of nutmeg.'

128 BERCY SAUCE

A simple sauce with an elegant flavour. Especially for fish dishes.

Cooking time 15—20 minutes *Serves* 4

1 oz. butter
1 dessertspoon finely chopped shallot or onion
$\frac{1}{4}$ pint dry white wine
$\frac{1}{4}$ pint liquor in which fish was poached (or fish stock — see Recipe 4)
beurre manié (see Recipe 129)
1 dessertspoon finely chopped parsley
seasoning to taste

Melt butter in a saucepan. Add shallot or onion and fry very gently until soft and transparent — the shallot or onion should not turn colour at all. Add wine and fish liquor or stock and boil steadily until liquid is reduced by half. Lower heat (sauce should now be simmering slowly, not boiling) and gradually beat in small pieces of beurre manié. Remove from heat and add parsley. Season to taste and serve straight away.

129 BEURRE MANIÉ (kneaded butter)

Although Beurre Manié is not, in itself, a sauce, it generally ends up in sauce sections because it is used to thicken sauces at the very last moment. Not the classic type in the previous sections (unless for some reason they are too thin and need rectifying) but the sort of thin sauces or gravies one has after cooking a stew or ragoût.

Put 1 oz. softened butter on to a plate. Using a fork, work in to it $\frac{3}{4}$ oz. flour — the finished mixture should be like a thick paste. Divide it up into little pieces. Remove the pan of stew or whatever from the heat. Add the small pieces of Beurre Manié and gently shake the pan (stirring could break up the meat) until the sauce has a bright gloss and has thickened. If the sauce is still too thin, repeat the whole process over again. Avoid re-boiling or the flavour of the dish will be spoiled. The amount of Beurre Manié given above should be sufficient to thicken $\frac{1}{2}$—$\frac{3}{4}$ pint of liquid.

If the Beurre Manié is used to thicken a sauce (such as a Brown Sauce) which is too thin, the pan of sauce should be kept over a low heat and small pieces of the Beurre Manié stirred in. The sauce shouldn't actually be re-boiled, but simmered just long enough to take away the raw taste of the flour.

BREAD SAUCE

Although we know that the art of bread-making is centuries old — it seems the Romans had bakeries for making leavened bread as early as 200 B C — it is difficult to trace Bread Sauce very far back in time. Certainly it was going strong well over 150 years ago, and it was probably eaten in one form or another much earlier. We do know that roast chicken and turkey wouldn't seem quite the same without the traditional sausage, roll of bacon and dollop of bread sauce on the sides of our plates!

From 'Domestic Cookery by a Lady' published about 1843, comes this recipe. 'Take a large onion, slice it down very thin, put it into some broth or water, let it boil until tender; add a sufficient quantity of breadcrumbs to thicken it, 2 oz. of butter, pepper, and salt, and a little good cream; boil it until it is thick and very smooth but do not allow it to be too thick to pour into a sauce tureen. This receipt is from the Palace, and comes highly recommended.'

Mrs. Rundell, who is the author of 'Domestic Cookery', included also the more familiar recipe using all milk, and Mrs. Beeton, too, gave one recipe using a home-made broth from poultry giblets and one using milk. Our old friend, Mr. Read, writing in 'The Cook', summed it all up very simply in his one recipe by saying, 'Bread sauce is either made with gravy or milk.'

My recipe is an all milk one; if preferred you could use good chicken stock only or half stock and half milk.

130 BREAD SAUCE

Cooking time 25—30 minutes   *Serves* 4—6

6 cloves
1 large onion, peeled
6 white peppercorns
1 blade mace or large pinch of ground nutmeg
1 small bay leaf
a sprig of parsley

½ pint milk
2 oz. fresh white bread-crumbs
½ oz. butter
3 tablespoons cream (single is good, double better!)
salt and pepper to taste

Press cloves half way into the onion. Put into a saucepan. Add the peppercorns, mace or nutmeg, bay leaf, parsley and milk. Bring just up to the boil and immediately lower the heat. Cover the pan and simmer *very slowly* for 20 minutes. Strain hot milk on to bread-crumbs. Add butter and cream. Mix thoroughly and return to low heat. Stir until sauce is smooth and fairly thick. Season to taste with salt and pepper and transfer to sauce-boat or dish. Serve with a small ladle or spoon.

131 BOURGUIGNONNE SAUCE

Sometimes known as Burgundy sauce. A hearty sauce with a fine bouquet and excellent for egg dishes and meat grills.

Cooking time 20—25 minutes   *Serves* 4

¾ pint red Burgundy
2 shallots or 1 small onion, finely chopped
1 tablespoon roughly chopped parsley
a good pinch of thyme

½ a small bay leaf
1 oz. mushroom stalks
beurre manié (see Recipe 129)
seasoning to taste

Put Burgundy into a saucepan. Add shallots or onion, parsley, thyme, bay leaf and mushroom stalks. Bring to the boil and simmer until the wine is reduced by half. Strain and pour into a clean saucepan. Just before serving, bring wine mixture just to the boil. Lower heat and gradually beat in small pieces of Beurre Manié. Season to taste and serve straight away.

132 CHESTNUT SAUCE

The Victorian Encyclopedia of Practical Cookery says, 'In France, the better kinds (of chestnut) are known as *marrons*, and the Continental cook prefers the best in the many flavoursome dishes to which they are adapted. Candied and as a stuffing or a sauce for boiled turkey, appear to be the chief culinary uses to which they are applied in this country (England).' Times haven't changed.

As a child, I remember roasting chestnuts round the fire in the winter and burning my fingers as I peeled them. Fortunately, we don't have to have burned fingers any more, or depend on the season, because dried chestnuts are available from many Continental shops and delicatessen all the year round. They work out cheaper than fresh ones because there's no waste and I use about 6—8 oz. dried chestnuts instead of 1 lb. of fresh. I soak them overnight in cold water and the next morning they are at least twice their original size; exactly like fresh chestnuts. Chestnut sauce is traditionally served with turkey but is just as good with poultry. Blanch and peel fresh chestnuts before use.

Cooking time $1\frac{1}{2}$—$1\frac{3}{4}$ hours *Serves* 4—6

8 oz. chestnuts, peeled (or 4 oz. dried)
$\frac{1}{2}$ pint chicken stock (home made or use a stock cube and water)
1 long strip of lemon peel
1 small peeled onion
2 level teaspoons cornflour
4 tablespoons single cream
salt and pepper to taste

Put the chestnuts into a saucepan with stock, lemon peel and onion. Bring slowly to the boil. Cover and simmer for $1\frac{1}{4}$—$1\frac{1}{2}$ hours when the nuts should be soft. Remove lemon peel and onion and rub sauce — with chestnuts — through a sieve. Return to clean saucepan. Add the cornflour mixed to a smooth paste with the cream. Return to a low heat and cook slowly, stirring continuously, until the sauce comes to the boil and thickens. Remove from heat and season to taste with salt and pepper.

CRANBERRY SAUCE

The cranberry as we know it today was originally christened Crane berry, partly because the pink blossom on the stems looked like the head of a crane and partly because the cranes themselves used to feast on the berries.

Cranberries are not new, and in the 'Fruit Manual', published in 1875, the author writes 'This (referring to the cranberry) grows abundantly in bogs or swamps, in many parts of England. The fruit is the size of a pea and the skin pale red; they have a somewhat acid flavour, and a strong acidity.'

Another book from the same period goes into more detail. 'They are so exceedingly prolific that it has been computed a piece of ground 18 foot square planted with either kind (the high berry or marsh berry) will produce enough fruit to make one hundred or more large pies. Cranberries grow abundantly in America, France and England, the small kind flourishing best in fenny districts and running water. There is a kind of cranberry grown in Northern Russia which, not withstanding its extreme acidity, is much used for making soups and sauces.'

One wonders what has happened to all the English cranberries that must have graced our tables a century ago because the bright red, plump and bouncy berries we see in our shops every winter come direct from America where they are very big business indeed. Cranberries are grown in New Jersey, Wisconsin, Oregon, and Washington and in Massachusetts they have Cranberry Houses which are gift shops, restaurants, experimental kitchens and bakeries, specifically for the cranberry industry, all rolled into one.

The old wooden cranberry scoops which were once used for harvesting the berries are now collectors' pieces and the pale, mauvy-pink and delicate cranberry glass ornaments, which were made between 1835 and 1870, are much sought-after antiques both in America and England.

The popularity of the American cranberry is largely due to its versatility — it goes with practically everything — its high vitamin C content, its bright colour and sweet-sour flavour. The Thanksgiving turkey is *always* served with Cranberry Sauce and in England more and more people are eating Cranberry Sauce, fresh or canned, with Christmas dinner or on any other occasion when they have poultry. Perhaps, in England, we will one day see the return of the home grown cranberry. In the meantime, we can still enjoy the imported ones which are sent to England from about September to December and which can be stored for an indefinite length of time in a well-maintained domestic deep freeze.

Fresh Cranberry Sauce is easy to make and fun to listen to because as the berries cook they burst open and make jolly little popping sounds! The sauce is traditionally eaten with turkey but goes equally well with pork, lamb, goose, duck, tongue, gammon, chicken and game. My husband loves it with canned milk pudding and it is delicious, hot or cold, as a sauce for apple pie and baked or steamed sponge puddings.

133 CRANBERRY SAUCE

Cooking time 14—16 minutes *Serves* 4—6

6 oz. granulated sugar   8 oz. fresh cranberries
¼ pint water

Put the sugar and water into a saucepan. Leave over
a low heat until sugar dissolves. Bring to the boil and
add the cranberries. Cook fairly rapidly until the skins
pop open; this takes 2—3 minutes. Lower heat and
continue to simmer for a further 7—8 minutes. Serve
hot or cold.

134 CRANBERRY AND APPLE SAUCE

A delicious sauce for roast pork, duck or goose.

Cooking time 16—20 minutes *Serves* 4—6

4 oz. cooking apples,   6 oz. granulated sugar
  weighed after peeling   4 oz. fresh cranberries
¼ pint water

Cut apples into thin slices. Put into a saucepan with
water. Cook over a low heat until apples are soft and
pulpy. Add sugar and stir until dissolved. Add cranberries and cook until the skins pop open. Lower heat
and cover pan. Simmer gently for a further 8 minutes.
Serve hot or cold.

135 CREOLE SAUCE

Creole food — which comes from the Mississippi Delta
or Deep South — is a mixture of French, Spanish and
negro cooking and is as warm and as vivid and as
exotic as the people themselves. Creole sauce — made
from tomatoes, garlic, onions, olives, green peppers,
spices and herbs — is a typical example of the style,

and if you want a colourful and sunset-red sauce to serve with shellfish, hard-boiled eggs, duck, pork, lamb and fluffy boiled rice, spare a little time to make the recipe below which always reminds me, nostalgically, of Scarlett O'Hara in 'Gone With the Wind'. I don't know why!

Cooking time 1 hour   *Serves* 6—8

1 oz. butter
2 teaspoons salad oil
1 large onion, very finely chopped
1 garlic clove, very finely chopped
2 oz. green olives, stoned and finely chopped
1 medium can (about 14 oz.) whole peeled tomatoes
$\frac{1}{2}$ small green pepper, very finely chopped

1 small bay leaf
$\frac{1}{4}$ level teaspoon basil
1 level dessertspoon very finely chopped parsley
2 level teaspoons brown sugar
$\frac{1}{2}$ level teaspoon salt
$\frac{1}{2}$—1 teaspoon Tabasco sauce
1 strip lemon peel, about 2 inches long
2 oz. mushrooms and stalks

Heat butter and oil in a saucepan. Add onion and garlic and fry very gently until soft but not brown. Add olives and fry another 2 minutes. Add all remaining ingredients and bring slowly to the boil, stirring continuously. Lower heat and cover pan. Simmer slowly, stirring occasionally, for about 50 minutes or until the sauce has boiled down and is thick. Remove the bay leaf and strip of lemon peel before serving.

136 CUMBERLAND SAUCE (HOT)

This is a full-bodied sauce flavoured with ginger, cloves, dry red wine or port, redcurrant jelly and orange and lemon peel. It is meant to be served with strong flavoured meats such as gammon and ham. It is also very good with smoked tongue and roast pork.

Cooking time 18—20 minutes   *Serves* 6

½ level teaspoon dry mustard

3 level dessertspoons soft brown sugar

large pinch of ginger

shake of cayenne pepper

¼ level teaspoon salt

½ pint dry red wine or port

2 cloves

1 level tablespoon cornflour

2 tablespoons cold water

4 tablespoons redcurrant jelly

1 level teaspoon finely grated lemon peel

1 level teaspoon finely grated orange peel

juice of 1 small orange

juice of 1 small lemon

Put mustard, sugar, ginger, pepper and salt into a saucepan. Mix to a smooth paste with a little of the wine. Stir in rest of wine. Add cloves and slowly bring mixture to boil, stirring continuously. Lower heat and cover pan. Simmer slowly for 10 minutes. Mix cornflour to a smooth cream with the cold water. Add to sauce and stir continuously until it thickens. Add all remaining ingredients and leave over a low heat until redcurrant jelly has melted and the sauce is hot. Season to taste before serving.

117

137 CUMBERLAND SAUCE (COLD)

This is slightly different from the hot version in that it is unthickened and strained before serving. It is specifically for cold ham, game and brawn.

Cooking time 25 minutes   *Serves* 4

$\frac{1}{4}$ pint dry red wine or port	1 small onion, very finely chopped
3 tablespoons redcurrant jelly	$\frac{1}{2}$ level teaspoon dry mustard
finely grated peel and juice of 1 medium lemon and of 1 medium orange	2 cloves
	pinch of ginger
	salt and pepper to taste

Put all the ingredients into a saucepan and slowly bring to boil, stirring all the time. Lower heat and cover pan. Simmer sauce very gently for 20 minutes. Strain and allow to cool completely before serving.

138 CURRANT SAUCE FOR VENISON OR PORK

Reminiscent of the good old days when dinners were banquets and when the gentlemen retired to the smoking room with large balloons of brandy, while the ladies chatted about *petit point* or the servants I suppose! This recipe comes from 'Domestic Cookery By a Lady' and I give it exactly as it was written. 'Clean an ounce of currants and boil them in $\frac{1}{2}$ pint of water for a few minutes, pour the whole over a tea-cupful of breadcrumbs; let it soak, and then add a piece of butter rolled in flour, 4 or 6 cloves, and a glass of port wine; beat it a little, and stir it over the fire until it is quite smooth.'

139 CURRY SAUCE

Curry sauce is useful if you want to make curries in a hurry and use up left-over meat, poultry or fish. A bed of rice, topped with hard-boiled eggs or pieces of vegetable, and coated with the sauce, makes an easy and inexpensive meal and even plain boiled rice, mixed with the sauce, can be served as a side dish to accompany meat, fish, egg or poultry dishes. I have given a flexible amount of curry to add, largely because a curry sauce is more personal than most in that some people like a hot, fiery flavour while others prefer a milder one.

Cooking time 1 hour

Serves 4

1 oz. butter
1 dessertspoon salad oil
1 large onion, very finely chopped
1 or 2 garlic cloves, very finely chopped
2—6 level dessertspoons curry powder
1 level tablespoon flour
3 level dessertspoons tomato purée
$\frac{1}{2}$ level teaspoon ginger
$\frac{1}{4}$ level teaspoon cinnamon
3 cloves

2 level tablespoons sweet pickle
$\frac{1}{2}$ level teaspoon salt
$\frac{1}{4}$—$\frac{1}{2}$ level teaspoon cayenne pepper (omit for mild sauce)
2 dessertspoons lemon juice
1 oz. desiccated coconut
$\frac{3}{4}$ pint boiling stock or water
1 oz. seedless raisins (optional)
1 small cooking apple, peeled and grated (optional)

Heat butter and oil in a saucepan. Add onion and garlic and fry gently until pale gold. Stir in curry powder, flour, purée, ginger, cinnamon, cloves, sweet pickle, salt, cayenne pepper (if used) and lemon juice. Leave over a very low heat. Add coconut to the boiling stock or water then strain into saucepan. Cook, stirring all the time, until sauce comes to boil and thickens.

Add raisins and apple (use these if you like a fruity-flavoured sauce, otherwise omit), lower heat and cover pan. Simmer *slowly* for 45 minutes, stirring occasionally. If a smooth sauce is preferred, strain and reheat before serving.

140 GOOSEBERRY SAUCE

This is an old English sauce, not often made any more. It used to be served with goose, duck and mackerel and is well worth reviving, especially when there are home-grown gooseberries in our back gardens and shops. About a hundred years ago there were as many as 224 varieties of gooseberries to choose from — red skinned, yellow, green or white skinned, some with hair and some without — and it's no wonder that the sauce was made more often then than it is today.

Cooking time about   *Serves* 4—6
   15 minutes

8 oz. cooking gooseberries, $\frac{1}{2}$ oz. butter
   topped and tailed   1—2 level tablespoons
2 tablespoons water   granulated sugar
$\frac{1}{2}$ level teaspoon finely grated
   lemon peel

Put gooseberries into a saucepan with the water. Bring to the boil. Lower heat and cover pan. Simmer slowly until fruit is soft and pulpy. Beat to a purée with the lemon peel and butter then sweeten to taste with the sugar; the sauce should be on the sharp side to counteract the richness of the birds or mackerel, so don't over-sweeten. Return to a low heat and stir until the sugar has completely dissolved. Serve hot or cold.

GRAVIES

Here are two gravies for those who like to make their own — without additions or colouring. It is usual to serve a fairly thin gravy with beef and poultry and a thicker one with lamb, veal and pork.

141 THIN GRAVY

Cooking time about   *Serves* 6
  6—7 minutes

pan juices (from roasting   ½ pint stock or water
  meat or poultry)   salt and pepper to taste
1 level dessertspoon flour

Pour off all but 3 dessertspoons of juice from the roasting tin. Stand tin over a low heat and stir in the flour. Cook until the mixture turns a warm brown, stirring all the time, so that the little crisp pieces of meat from the base of the tin are well mixed in. Gradually blend in stock or water. Cook, stirring continuously, until gravy comes to the boil and thickens. Simmer slowly for 2 minutes then season to taste with salt and pepper. Pour into a sauce-boat and serve straight away.

142 THICK GRAVY

Make in exactly the same way as the Thin Gravy (see Recipe 141) but increase the flour to 2 level dessertspoons.

143 GRILL SAUCE

A Victorian sauce for grilled meats. Very good as it stands but if you enjoy the combination of meat and fish, then you can add ½ teaspoon of anchovy essence or 1 or 2 finely chopped anchovy fillets instead.

A little goes a long way, hence the small quantity of ingredients.

Cooking time 2—3 minutes   *Serves* 3—4

1 tablespoon tomato ketchup
1 tablespoon wine vinegar
2 tablespoons double cream
½—1 teaspoon made
  mustard

½ teaspoon Worcestershire
  sauce
a shake of cayenne pepper

Mix all the ingredients well together. Heat through gently without boiling and serve straight away.

144 HORSERADISH RELISH

A popular sauce for hot roast beef and cold smoked trout.

Cooking time nil   *Serves* 4—6

¼ pint double cream
2 tablespoons cold milk
2 teaspoons lemon juice
1 teaspoon wine vinegar
2 level tablespoons finely
  grated horseradish

¼—½ level teaspoon salt
½—1 level teaspoon sifted
  icing sugar
a shake of pepper

Whip cream and milk together until stiff. Stir in all remaining ingredients.

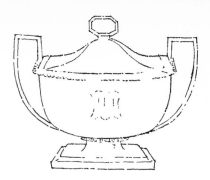

MARINADES

The Marinade, according to a Victorian authority, 'is a French culinary term which signifies a souse, brine or pickle, in which fish, flesh or fowl may be soaked (*mariné*) for a period preparatory to their being cooked. By this means a considerable addition is made to the natural flavour of the article being marinaded.' What the author didn't add was that in the days before refrigeration, Marinades were frequently used not so much to add flavour but to mask the flavour and aroma coming from foods that were going off!

Now that we have more or less overcome the problem of stale foods, Marinades serve three basic functions. One is to tenderise raw meat and poultry, the second is to keep the food a good colour and the third is to give a flavour lift to foods which might otherwise be tasteless. Marinades don't start off as sauces, but frequently the foods themselves are cooked in the Marinades and the resultant pan juices are either thickened and used as a sauce or boiled down to half or even a quarter of their original quantity and then added to the sauce to accentuate its flavour.

Because of their acid content, Marinades should be put into a glass, earthenware, stainless steel or enamel dish and the food in the Marinade stirred with a wooden spoon or fork, not a metal one.

As Marinades are very well-seasoned and spiced and as most poultry, meat and fish absorb flavours fairly readily, don't overdo the soaking time or the flavour of the dish may be spoilt. Small cubes of meat and cutlets should be marinated for about $2\frac{1}{2}$—3 hours and whole, large joints — such as a leg of lamb or pork — can be left in a Marinade overnight. The food should be turned in the Marinade occasionally and kept refrigerated or in the coldest part of the larder to prevent deterioration.

145 BACON MARINADE

Particularly good for joints of lamb, pork and veal.

Cooking time nil

8 tablespoons salad oil	1 tablespoon coarsely chopped parsley
2 tablespoons vinegar	
2 tablespoons lemon juice	$\frac{1}{2}$ level teaspoon mixed herbs
2 oz. finely chopped streaky bacon	$\frac{1}{2}$ level teaspoon salt
1 or 2 finely chopped garlic cloves	

Beat oil, vinegar and lemon juice well together. Stir in remaining ingredients. Pour into bowl, dish or enamel plate. Add meat and coat well with the Marinade. Leave in the cold for approximately 4—6 hours or overnight if preferred.

146 ORANGE AND LEMON MARINADE

Suitable for small or large pieces of lamb, veal, pork, poultry and fish.

Cooking time nil

$\frac{1}{4}$ pint salad oil

4 tablespoons wine vinegar

2 tablespoons lemon juice

2 tablespoons orange juice

$\frac{1}{2}$—1 level teaspoon salt

$\frac{1}{4}$ level teaspoon cayenne pepper

$\frac{1}{2}$ level teaspoon finely grated lemon peel

$\frac{1}{2}$ level teaspoon finely grated orange peel

$\frac{1}{2}$ level teaspoon mixed herbs

Beat oil well together with vinegar, lemon and orange juice and salt. Stir in remaining ingredients. Pour into bowl, dish or enamel plate. Add meat, poultry or fish and coat well with the Marinade. Leave in the cold for a minimum of 6 hours.

147 WINE MARINADE

Especially good for joints of red meat and thick rump or porterhouse steaks.

Cooking time 20—30 minutes

¼ pint water
¼ pint dry red wine
1 large onion, thinly sliced
1 large carrot, thinly sliced
2 level tablespoons coarsely chopped parsley

6 peppercorns
1 bay leaf
1 chopped garlic clove
½ level teaspoon salt

Put all ingredients into a saucepan. Slowly bring to boil then lower heat. Simmer, uncovered, until liquid is reduced by a third. Strain, leave until completely cold. Pour into an earthenware bowl or dish. Add meat and coat well with Marinade. Leave in the cold overnight.

148 SPICED WHITE WINE MARINADE

An all-purpose Marinade that can be used for poultry, any type of meat and fish.

1 large onion, sliced
½ large lemon, sliced
2 bay leaves, broken up into small pieces
6 whole peppercorns
4 cloves

2 blades of mace
2 tablespoons coarsely chopped parsley
4 tablespoons olive oil
¼ pint dry white wine

Put onion and lemon into a bowl or dish. Add all remaining ingredients and stir well to mix. Add poultry, meat or fish and coat well with Marinade. Leave in the cold for a minimum of 3 hours and for a maximum of 6.

149 CIDER MARINADE

A fine-flavoured Marinade that is particularly recommended for fish. This is the type of Marinade in which the fish may be poached and the liquid subsequently thickened and used as a sauce.

Cooking time 1½ hours

3 medium onions
1 garlic clove (optional)
2 medium carrots
1 heaped tablespoon parsley
2 tablespoons salad oil

1 pint cider
1 tablespoon mixed pickling spice
2 cloves
1 level teaspoon salt

Chop the onions and garlic (if used) finely. Slice the carrots thinly. Coarsely chop the parsley. Heat the oil in a saucepan. Add the vegetables and parsley. Cover the pan and fry gently for 10 minutes, shaking the pan frequently. Add all remaining ingredients. Bring to the boil and boil for 5 minutes. Lower heat and simmer gently for 1¼ hours. Strain into a bowl and leave until completely cold. Add fish and leave to soak in the cool for 2—3 hours. Afterwards poach the fish in the Marinade.

As the Marinade keeps well, it may be strained after use, refrigeratored up to 3 days and used again.

150 VICTORIAN MARINADE FOR GAME

'Put into a saucepan one bottle of white wine, one pint of vinegar, one quart of water, one handful of peppercorns, four bay leaves, a few lumps of sugar, a slice or two of carrot and onion, and a root of parsley; boil up well, turn the Marinade into an earthenware pan, and it is ready for use. All large game should be left in a Marinade at least two days before cooking and should be turned in it once or twice a day.'

151 MINT SAUCE

Also from the same informative Encyclopedia, comes this explanation on the subject of mint. 'This is one of the most powerful herbs (*mentha veridis*) used in cookery. ...The name *mentha* is derived from the Greek Mintha, a daughter of Cocytus, who was metamorphosed into a mint-plant by Proserpine, doubtless from motives of jealousy. So powerful and characteristic is the flavour of mint, that cooks almost fear to venture its introduction into anything other than a vinegar sauce for lamb; but that it is capable of many other uses is shown by the following receipts. It should be used fresh if possible, for when dried it loses much of its flavour.'

For the purpose of this book, I will stick to the sauce only.

Cooking time nil

Serves 4

4 level tablespoons very finely chopped mint

2 tablespoons malt or wine vinegar

2–3 level teaspoons granulated or castor sugar

2 tablespoons boiling water

Put mint into basin. Add water and sugar and stir until the sugar dissolves. Leave until cold then stir in the vinegar.

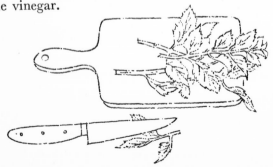

152 NEWBURG SAUCE

Although Newburg Sauce is generally considered to be a lobster sauce, this adaptation — which is very rich, creamy and beautifully flavoured — can be served with all shellfish and is one of those special occasion efforts that one likes to have up one's sleeve.

Cooking time 15—17 minutes *Serves* 4

1 oz. butter	3 egg yolks
2 level teaspoons finely grated onion	3—4 tablespoons dry sherry or Madeira
1 oz. flour	salt and pepper to taste
½ pint single cream	

Melt the butter in a heavy-based saucepan. Add the onion and fry very gently until soft but not brown. Add flour and cook over a low heat for 2 minutes, stirring all the time. On no account let the mixture of butter and flour (roux) turn colour. Remove from heat and gradually add cream, beating thoroughly after each addition. When sauce is smooth and completely lumpfree, bring slowly to the boil, stirring continuously. Simmer for 4 minutes then remove from heat. Put egg yolks and sherry or Madeira into a basin and whisk lightly until well mixed. Gradually beat in the sauce and pour back into saucepan. Cook over a low heat, stirring all the time, until the sauce is thick and smooth, but do not allow to boil. Season.

153 PANADA

Panada is a Spanish word derived from the Latin *panis*, meaning bread. At one time the Panada was simply bread pulp, made from bread and water boiled up together. Panadas in the modern sense are very thick sauces — usually white — which are used mainly as a binding ingredient for croquettes and similar mixtures, and as the basic sauce in soufflés. Because of their thickness, they are never used for coating foods.

Panadas are made with a roux of fat — mostly butter or margarine — plus flour and milk. When they are required for sweet dishes, omit the pepper.

Cooking time 10—12 minutes

2 oz. butter or margarine	salt and pepper to taste
2 oz. flour	½ pint cold milk

Melt fats in a heavy-based saucepan. Stir in the flour and seasonings and cook for 3 minutes, stirring continuously. Do not allow the roux to brown. Remove from heat and gradually add the milk, beating well after each addition. When the sauce is smooth and completely lump-free, bring slowly to the boil, stirring all the time. Continue to cook for a further 3—4 minutes or until the sauce is very thick; sufficiently so as to leave the sides of the pan clean and to form a ball in the centre. Use as required.

154 RAISIN SAUCE

A fruit sauce for those who like fruit and meat combinations. I always make this sauce with apple juice and add a very small amount of finely grated orange peel for good measure. The sauce goes well with ham, smoked tongue, roast lamb, goose or duck.

Cooking time 25 minutes   *Serves* 4—6

2 oz. seedless raisins	2 oz. soft brown sugar
½ pint apple juice	2 tablespoons orange juice
3 cloves	½ oz. butter
½ level teaspoon finely grated orange peel	1 or 2 dessertspoons Calvados (optional)
1 level tablespoon cornflour	

Put raisins into a saucepan. Add apple juice, cloves and orange peel. Bring to the boil and lower heat. Cover pan and simmer for 15 minutes. Mix cornflour and sugar to a smooth paste with the orange juice. Add to pan with butter. Cook, stirring, until mixture comes to the boil and thickens. Simmer for 2—3 minutes then stir in Calvados (if used). Serve straight away.

155 SAUCE OF CHIVES

A hundred-year-old recipe for a simple but interesting sauce which can be served with rabbit or hare. 'Put one teacupful of breadcrumbs into a saucepan, and stir over the fire until a pale golden colour; then pour in ½ pint broth (*I would recommend beef or chicken stock instead*) with two tablespoons of finely minced chives, and season to taste with salt. Stir the sauce over the fire till boiling, keeping it very smooth. It is then ready for serving.'

Another recipe from the same book is this one which would be delicious with poultry and poached or steamed white fish dishes. 'Put the yolks of four hard-boiled eggs in the mortar with one teaspoonful of dry mustard and one teaspoonful of sugar, and pound them until quite smooth. Finely chop a handful of fresh green chives, and mix them with the pounded eggs; then stir the mixture to a smooth, creamy sauce with one teacup of vinegar and one tablespoon of salad oil, and it is ready for serving.'

SWEET-SOUR SAUCES

Sweet-sour sauce invariably means the inclusion of an acid, such as vinegar or lemon juice, and sugar which is either white or brown depending on the dish being made. Although sweet-sour sauces are generally thought of as Chinese in origin, which they may be, many European countries also enjoy sweet-sour combinations of meat and fish. Germany's Sauerbraten is a well-known example and in Eastern Europe fish with sweet-sour sauce is much favoured. In Chinese cooking itself, vegetables, such as cabbage, green beans, celery and carrots, are frequently mixed with a sweet-sour sauce and Chinese Sweet-sour Pork, eaten more outside China than in it, has become a great favourite everywhere.

156 SWEET-SOUR SAUCE FOR VEGETABLES

A very simple sauce for hot cooked beetroots and lightly cooked and still-crisp cabbage, cauliflower, carrot slices, celery and green beans.

Cooking time 10 minutes *Serves* 4

6 tablespoons wine or cider vinegar
5 tablespoons granulated sugar

pinch of salt
2 level teaspoons cornflour
1 tablespoon cold water
$\frac{1}{2}$ oz. butter

Put the vinegar, sugar and salt into a saucepan. Stand over a low heat until sugar dissolves; bring slowly to boil, stirring continuously. Mix cornflour to a smooth paste with the cold water. Add to saucepan. Cook, stirring all the time, until the sauce comes to the boil and thickens. Simmer for 3 minutes. Remove from heat, add butter and stir until melted. Serve hot.

157 SWEET-SOUR SAUCE FOR PORK

A typical Chinese-style sauce which contains soy sauce, green pepper, pineapple pieces and orange juice. I like to make the sauce with fresh pineapple, but when it is out of season, the canned variety makes an excellent substitute.

Cooking time 15 minutes   *Serves* 6—8

3 level dessertspoons cornflour
2 tablespoons cold water
$\frac{1}{2}$ pint chicken stock
1 oz. butter
1 medium green pepper cut into small squares
4 pineapple slices, fresh or canned

$\frac{1}{4}$ pint wine or cider vinegar
juice of 1 large orange
4 oz. castor sugar
$\frac{1}{4}$ level teaspoon ginger
$\frac{1}{2}$ level teaspoon salt
2 tablespoons soy sauce

Mix the cornflour to a smooth paste with the cold water. Put the chicken stock, butter and green pepper into a saucepan. Chop the pineapple coarsely and add to pan. Bring to boil and lower heat. Cover pan and simmer for 5 minutes. Add the cornflour paste and all remaining ingredients. Cook gently, stirring all the time, until the sugar dissolves and the sauce comes to the boil and thickens. Simmer for 2 minutes, pour over deep-fried pork in batter and serve immediately.

158 SWEET-SOUR SAUCE FOR FISH

Also known as Egg and Lemon Sauce, this is typically Jewish with a light, refreshing flavour. It is always served cold over poached fish — usually mackerel or halibut — and the consistency is on the thin side, rather like a pouring sauce.

Cooking time about 6—7 minutes

Serves 4

2 level teaspoons cornflour or potato flour
juice of 1 medium lemon
¼ pint liquor in which the fish was poached

2 egg yolks
seasoning to taste

Mix the cornflour or potato flour to a smooth paste with the lemon juice. Gradually blend in the fish liquor. Pour into a saucepan. Cook slowly, stirring all the time, until the sauce comes to the boil and thickens. Simmer for 1 minute and remove from heat. Immediately beat in egg yolks and season to taste with salt and pepper. Pour over the fish (which should be on a serving platter) and leave until cold. If put in fridge, remove an hour before serving.

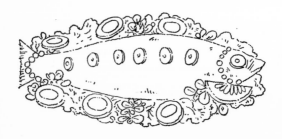

TOMATO SAUCE

The tomato, which is known as the love apple and apple of Paradise, is said to be a native of South America and Mexico and was supposed to have been introduced to the West Indies by the Spaniards. It reached Europe and England round about 1596 and its almost universal cultivation has been going on steadily ever since.

About 150 years ago the tomato was, in England at any rate, regarded with a measure of suspicion. 'The whole plant has a disagreeable odour, and its juice, subjected to the action of the fire, emits a vapour so powerful as to cause vertigo and vomiting.' A Mrs. Beeton comment.

Another book of the same period says this. 'Now that their agreeable qualities are better known, they are beginning to be more generally appreciated with us, and, in addition to those grown in this country, considerable quantities are imported from the Continent. Tomatoes, although associated in kind with poisonous plants, are perfectly wholesome as food, and may be eaten freely without fear of injury; indeed they are supposed to exercise a healthful influence over the liver and other organs.'

The Victorians always referred to tomatoes as fruit and the red ones were candied in sugar and treated as confectionery or made into an assortment of jams and preserves. The fate of the green ones was much the same then as it is today — they ended up in the pickle pan and were made into chutney!

When tomatoes are used in cooking they should be skinned first (no one enjoys finding bits of tomato skin in their sauce) and there are two ways of doing this. A very quick one, for those with gas cookers, is to spear the tomato on to a fork and stand it over the gas flames, as near to them as possible. The tomato skin will split and char rapidly and subsequently slide off the tomato with the greatest of ease. The second and more conventional method is this. Put the tomatoes into a basin and cover them with boiling water. Leave for 3 minutes and drain. Slide off the skins then plunge the tomatoes straight into a bowl of cold water, so that they become firm again and lose their flabbiness.

159 FRESH TOMATO SAUCE (1)

A versatile and all-purpose sauce — which is also known as Portugaise sauce — that goes with practically all savoury dishes whether they are made from meat, poultry, fish or eggs.

Cooking time 1 hour   *Serves* 6

2 tablespoons salad oil	$\frac{1}{4}$ pint stock or water
1 medium onion, very finely chopped	1 small bay leaf
1—2 oz. bacon scraps	2 cloves
1 finely chopped garlic clove (optional)	4 white peppercorns
1 small carrot, thinly sliced	a large pinch of basil
1 oz. flour	1 level dessertspoon soft brown or Demerara sugar
12 oz. tomatoes, skinned and chopped	$\frac{1}{2}$ level teaspoon salt
3 level tablespoons tomato purée	a 2-inch strip of lemon peel
	2 teaspoons lemon juice or wine vinegar
	pepper to taste

Heat the oil in a large, heavy-based saucepan. Add onion, bacon scraps, garlic (if used) and the carrot. Cover pan and fry gently for about 7 minutes, shaking the pan frequently. Stir in the flour then add the tomatoes and tomato purée. Gradually blend in stock or water. Cook, stirring continuously, until the sauce

comes to the boil and thickens. Add all remaining ingredients and simmer the sauce for 45 minutes, stirring frequently as tomato mixtures have a habit of sticking. Strain sauce and return to a clean saucepan. Season to taste and reheat before serving.

160 TOMATO SAUCE (2)

This sauce uses canned tomatoes, lovely elongated ones from Italy that come already skinned, and it is a bit peasant style; rough and rugged because it is unstrained. It is flavoured with celery and mace and is a comfortable sauce to serve with poultry and lamb roasts and is a favourite of mine with roast duck and thick, freshly grilled gammon steaks.

Cooking time 1 hour   *Serves* 6

2 tablespoons salad oil
1 medium onion, very finely chopped
2 medium celery stalks, finely chopped
1 oz. lean bacon, finely chopped
1 small carrot, grated
1 oz. flour

1 can (about 14—15 oz.) Italian peeled tomatoes
2 level tablespoons tomato purée
1 blade of mace
½ level teaspoon salt
¼ pint stock or water
2 level teaspoons castor sugar

137

Heat oil in a large saucepan. Add the onion, celery, bacon and carrot. Cover pan and fry gently for about 7 minutes, shaking the pan frequently. Stir in the flour then add the tomatoes, purée, mace, salt and stock or water. Bring to the boil, stirring continuously, then add the sugar. Lower heat and cover pan. Simmer the sauce gently for 45 minutes, stirring frequently. Remove the mace before serving and season to taste.

VICTORIAN SAUCES

These are interesting and would be amusing to make at home if one had a bit of spare time; rather like making one's own wine! They are really bottled sauces, similar to the bottled ketchups that are so familiar and widely used today, and their purpose was the same in Victorian times as it is now; to season foods which have no accompanying sauces.

Although ketchup is either Chinese and/or Japanese in origin, it is from Britain that the large variety of different flavoured ketchups came. Continental cooks considered ketchup to be a 'piquant sauce made from mushrooms' while in Britain ketchup was being 'brewed' from a vast assortment of ingredients which included anchovies, cockles, cucumbers, elderberries, mussels, oysters, peppers, tomatoes, walnuts and wine. Some of the recipes were very complicated indeed and contained ingredients which are no longer readily available. Others were much simpler and it is these I give below with a final word from the author of the Victorian cookery book from which these came. 'The following receipts are highly recommended, and they will be found ample for all purposes requiring bottled sauces, but in the cases of those sauces having proprietary names, the receipts should be considered as merely approximate to the originals or good imitations.'

138

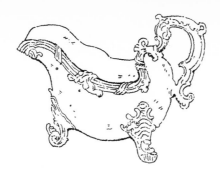

161 CAMP KETCHUP

Put 2 quarts of old beer and half the quantity of white wine in a saucepan with 4 oz. of anchovies, place it on the fire, and when at boiling-point take it off, add 3 oz. peeled shallots and ½ oz. each of ginger, nutmeg, mace, and pepper and let it remain for a fortnight, shaking it frequently. When settled, filter, and bottle the clear liquid, it is then ready for use. It will keep good for several years.

162 UNIVERSAL SAUCE

Put into a stew pan an equal quantity of broth and white wine, add two bay leaves, the thinly pared rind of a lemon, and a little pepper and salt. When on the point of boiling, move the stew pan to the edge of the fire, and let the contents simmer for 3 hours. Strain the sauce, mix it with the strained juice of a lemon, and bottle. It is then ready for use.

163 WORCESTERSHIRE SAUCE

Put ½ oz. each of ground shallots, garlic, and cayenne pepper into an earthenware jar, pour in 1 quart of white wine vinegar; let these get well incorporated; add one teacup of soy sauce, and bottle for future use.

164 HOT SAUCE

Mix together ¾ oz. of cayenne pepper, 2 tablespoons of soy sauce, four anchovies, three cloves of garlic, and one shallot. Pound (or chop) the above ingredients, and rub them through a fine hair sieve, then mix them with one quart of vinegar. Strain the sauce, pour into a bottle, and cork it down tightly. In a fortnight's time, the sauce will be fit for use.

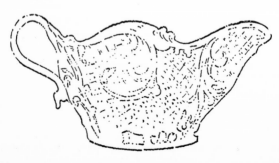

Quick Sauces

If one is a sauce enthusiast at all, one would like always to have time to make sauces from scratch and not fall back on, or make do with, substitutes. Alas, unexpectedly confronted with a handful of guests for a meal, there is probably no time to prepare anything other than a cold Blender Mayonnaise or a Hollandaise Sauce and even those may be too much of a good thing (especially if everyone's milling about in the kitchen trying to help!) or quite unsuitable for the food you are going to serve. Faced with an emergency like this, and it happens to all of us, I must confess I do turn to canned condensed soups because with one or other of them I can whisk up a sauce in a matter of minutes without wondering if I've the right ingredients in the cupboard, and whether there will be enough milk left for coffee; I don't have to keep the guests waiting too long for their food and I can get out of the kitchen quickly and at least be sociable!

A can of condensed mushroom or tomato soup has saved me going into a panic on many occasions and with the addition of the odd dash of wine or sherry, the tablespoon of cream, the shake of spice and pinch of herbs, I've turned out some splendid emergency sauces and saved the day handsomely! One thing is important regarding sauces made from condensed soups — they are inclined to be already well salted.

165 SAUCE À LA KING

One of my favourite quickies is the North American standby called Sauce à la King. It is made with a can of condensed mushroom soup and red or green pepper (I use dried pepper flakes for speed) and can have any number of additions; I add cream, butter, egg yolk, sherry and a pinch of nutmeg. To make a meal with the sauce, I include anything to hand, bite-sized pieces of cold cooked chicken or turkey; hard-boiled eggs cut into quarters, a can of drained and flaked tuna or salmon. In just a brief time, I have the beginnings of a very tasty main dish and all it needs is a packet of freshly cooked flat noodles to complete it.

Cooking time 8—9 minutes   *Serves* 4—6

1 level tablespoon dried pepper flakes	1 tablespoon dry sherry or lemon juice
boiling water	1 egg yolk
$\frac{1}{2}$ oz. butter	2 or 3 tablespoons single or double cream
1 can (10$\frac{1}{2}$ oz.) condensed mushroom soup	a large pinch of nutmeg
$\frac{1}{4}$ pint milk	pepper to taste

Cover the pepper flakes with boiling water and leave for 2 minutes. Drain thoroughly. Heat the butter in a saucepan. Add the pepper flakes and fry gently for 1 minute. Stir in the soup and milk and continue stirring over a low heat until the sauce is smooth. Simmer until hot. Meanwhile beat sherry, egg yolk and cream well together. Add to the hot sauce and stir until thoroughly mixed. Add nutmeg and pepper to taste and reheat sauce without boiling.

166 MACARONI CHEESE AND MUSHROOM SAUCE

A useful sauce if you want to make a speedy macaroni cheese-type dish that is a bit different from usual. Choose quick cooking macaroni and the whole thing can be ready in about 20 minutes.

Cooking time 6 minutes   *Serves* 4

1 can (10½ oz.) condensed cream of mushroom soup
¼ pint milk
½ level teaspoon made mustard

2—3 oz. Cheddar cheese, finely grated
pepper to taste

Put the soup and milk into a saucepan and cook over a low heat, stirring continuously, until the sauce is smooth and hot. Add mustard and cheese and stir until cheese melts. Add pepper to taste and use as required.

167 CELERY SAUCE FOR FISH

This is a delicate, mild and creamy sauce for all baked, poached, steamed and grilled white fish dishes and goes very well also with hot crab.

Cooking time 6 minutes   *Serves* 4—6

1 can (10½ oz.) condensed cream of celery soup
5 tablespoons double cream
1 oz. butter (unsalted for preference)

2 tablespoons dry white wine
½ level teaspoon paprika
pepper to taste

Put the soup and cream into a saucepan and cook over a low heat, stirring continuously, until the sauce is smooth and hot. Add all remaining ingredients and leave over a low heat until the butter melts, stirring frequently. Serve straight away.

168 CHICKEN AND ALMOND SAUCE

A rather luxurious and special occasion sauce for roast chicken, turkey and veal.

Cooking time 10 minutes   *Serves* 4—6

1 oz. flaked almonds
1 oz. butter (unsalted for preference)
1 can (10½ oz.) condensed cream of chicken soup

4 tablespoons single cream
2 tablespoons dry cider or white wine
pepper to taste

Fry the almonds gently in the butter until pale gold then remove from heat. Put soup and cream into a saucepan and cook over a low heat, stirring continuously, until the sauce is smooth and hot. Add almonds (with any remaining butter from the pan), cider or wine and pepper to taste. Reheat, stirring frequently, until the sauce is hot and smooth, but do not allow to boil.

169 QUICK CREOLE-STYLE SAUCE

An easy imitation of the original which is pleasant with lamb grills and roasts, roast duck and goose, pork grills and roasts, roast chicken, fried veal and hard-boiled eggs.

Cooking time 10 minutes   *Serves* 4—6

2 level tablespoons dried pepper flakes	$\frac{1}{4}$—$\frac{1}{2}$ level teaspoon dried basil or oregano
boiling water	1 level teaspoon granulated sugar
1 can (10$\frac{1}{2}$ oz.) condensed tomato soup	1 teaspoon Worcestershire sauce
5 tablespoons water	
2 oz. stuffed olives, sliced	

Cover the pepper flakes with boiling water and leave for 2 minutes. Drain thoroughly. Put soup into a saucepan with the water and cook over a low heat, stirring continuously, until sauce is smooth and hot. Add pepper flakes and all remaining ingredients and cover pan. Simmer for 7 minutes, stirring occasionally.

170 QUICK PIQUANT SAUCE

A good one for beef grills and roasts, boiled tongue and beef, corned beef fritters, toad-in-the-hole, fried or grilled sausages and boiled bacon.

Cooking time 10 minutes   *Serves* 4—6

1 can (10$\frac{1}{2}$ oz.) condensed oxtail soup	1 level tablespoon drained and finely chopped capers
5 tablespoons water	$\frac{1}{2}$ level teaspoon mixed herbs
2 level tablespoons finely chopped parsley	1 tablespoon dry sherry
1 level tablespoon finely chopped gherkins	1 teaspoon Worcestershire sauce
	pepper to taste

Put the soup and water into a saucepan and cook over a low heat, stirring continuously, until the sauce is hot and smooth. Add all remaining ingredients and bring sauce just to the boil, stirring all the time. Lower heat, cover pan and simmer gently for 5 minutes.

145

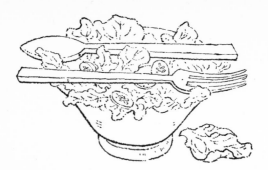

Salad Dressings

Reading through my early Mrs. Beeton I came across this poem on salads, with dressings included, which seemed an appropriate way of beginning this chapter: 'The Reverend Sidney Smith, the witty canon of St. Paul's, who thought that an enjoyment of the good things of this earth was compatible with aspirations for things higher, wrote the following excellent recipe for salad, which we would advise our readers not to pass by without a trial when the hot weather invites to a dish of cold lamb. May they find the flavour equal to the rhyme!'

'Two large potatoes, pass'd through kitchen sieve,
Smoothness and softness to the salad give;
Of mordent mustard add a single spoon,
Distrust the condiment that bites too soon;
But deem it not, thou man of herbs, a fault,
To add a double quantity of salt.
Four times the spoon with oil of Lucca crown,
And twice with vinegar procured from "town"
True flavour needs it, and your poet begs,
The pounded yellow of two well-boiled eggs.

Let onion's atoms lurk within the bowl,
And, scarce suspected, animate the whole;
And, lastly, in the flavour'd compound toss
A magic spoonful of anchovy sauce.
Oh! Great and glorious, and herbaceous treat,
'Twould tempt the dying anchorite to eat.
Back to the world he'd turn his weary soul,
And plunge his fingers in the salad-bowl.'

In a book called 'Gothic England' by John Harvey, published in 1948, there are some fascinating references to food customs in the early part of the 15th century and in one of them we are given a recipe for salad which shows how, in the absence of salad greens as we know them today, vegetables of the onion family and assorted herbs were used instead. But even though salads from those days were quite different from the ones we eat now, oil and vinegar — with a dash of salt — were still used as a dressing although they were probably not beaten together. The salad was mixed with oil and the vinegar was added afterwards. 'Take parsel, sawge, garlec, chibollas (young onions), oynons, leek, borage, myntes, porrectes (leaves of onion or leek?), fenel, and ton tressis (cresses), rew, rosemarye, purslarye (purslane); lave, and waishe hem clene; pike hem, pluk hem small with thyn honde, and myng hem wel with rawe oile. Lay on vynegar and salt, and serve it forth.'

We have the luxury-loving King Henry VIII and his wife Queen Katharine to thank for bringing carrots, cabbage, radishes and salad greens to England. At that period in history these vegetables were grown only in Holland so the enterprising king, whether to please himself or his wife is uncertain, imported a Dutch gardener specially to cultivate these rarities in England. The gardener was obviously successful (which was just as well in view of the king's temperament!) and as a result we have enjoyed salads for many hundreds of years.

The salad dressing in its simplest form is a mixture of oil and acid — vinegar or lemon juice — seasoned to taste with salt and pepper and sometimes English or Continental mustard. The oil can be olive, corn or groundnut and the acid must be the very finest wine or cider vinegar — never malt vinegar, it's too harsh — or fresh lemon juice.

The object of a dressing is to lubricate and bring out the flavours of the delicate salad ingredients and the dressing itself can be either subtle and mild or strong and full of zest, depending on personal taste. Very often the dressing may be so seasoned as to emphasise the main dish. For example, horseradish may be included in the dressing for beef salad and Parmesan cheese if you are serving side salads to accompany Italian-style spaghetti or macaroni dishes. The proportion of oil to acid is fairly standard; in general it is 2 parts oil to 1 of vinegar or lemon juice although on the Continent, where an oilier dressing is preferred, as much as 3 or even 4 parts of oil to acid are used, and the oil is usually olive; rarely any other.

Salad dressings are easy and uncomplicated to make. The oil is well beaten with the seasonings and then the acid is beaten in until the dressing thickens slightly and forms an emulsion. To make a salad dressing quickly, the oil and seasonings should be put into a screw-topped bottle and shaken well. The acid should then be added and the bottle shaken vigorously until the dressing thickens slightly. Alternatively, all the ingredients may be put into a blender for 15—20 seconds or until the dressing becomes a smooth emulsion.

Dressing may be made in quantity, poured into a jar with a lid and kept refrigerated until required. Then it is a simple matter of taking as much as you need and adding any additions you fancy to give different flavoured dressings. One word of warning. Flavouring such as fresh herbs and garlic spoil a dressing if they are allowed to remain in it for too long. Garlic cloves should, therefore, be left in the dressing for no longer than 24 hours while herbs and other flavourings should be beaten into the dressing just prior to using.

Green and mixed salads should be tossed with dressing immediately before serving. If the dressing is added way ahead of time, the greenery will become limp, soggy and acid and completely lose its fresh crispness. When dressing is added to a tossed, mixed or green salad, there should be just enough to coat the leaves and additions; not so much that there is a pool left behind in the bottom of the salad bowl.

171 CLASSIC FRENCH DRESSING

Suitable for all green and mixed salads, rice salads, tomato salads and for serving with avocado pears, cold artichoke hearts and cold asparagus.

Cooking time nil

3—4 tablespoons olive oil (or other oil to taste)	a pinch of castor sugar
$\frac{1}{4}$ level teaspoon salt	1 tablespoon wine or cider vinegar or lemon juice
a shake of white pepper	

Put the oil, salt, pepper and sugar into a small basin. Beat until well mixed. Gradually beat in vinegar or lemon juice and use as required.

172 VINAIGRETTE DRESSING

Also frequently known as French Dressing. This is a more flavoursome dressing than the Classic one (see Recipe 171) and may be used for all salads, avocado pears, cold artichoke hearts and cold asparagus.

Cooking time nil

3—4 tablespoons olive oil (or other oil to taste)
$\frac{1}{4}$ level teaspoon salt
$\frac{1}{4}$ level teaspoon dry mustard or $\frac{1}{2}$ level teaspoon Continental mustard
$\frac{1}{2}$ level teaspoon castor sugar or 1 coffee spoon of golden syrup

a shake of white pepper
3—4 drops Worcestershire sauce (optional)
$1\frac{1}{2}$—2 tablespoons wine or cider vinegar or lemon juice

Put the oil, salt, mustard, sugar or syrup, pepper and Worcestershire sauce into a basin. Beat until well mixed. Gradually beat in vinegar or lemon juice and use as required.

173 BLUE CHEESE DRESSING

A dressing flavoured with blue vein cheese (Danish blue, Stilton, Gorgonzola or Roquefort) which adds an unusual and different touch to all green and mixed salads, tomato salads and hard-boiled egg salads.

Cooking time nil

1 oz. blue vein cheese
3—4 tablespoons olive oil (or other oil to taste)
2—3 drops Worcestershire sauce

a light shake of pepper and salt
a large pinch of castor sugar
$1\frac{1}{2}$—2 tablespoons wine or cider vinegar or lemon juice

Put the cheese into a small basin and mash very finely. Gradually beat in oil, Worcestershire sauce, pepper, salt and sugar. When mixture is smooth and well blended, slowly beat in vinegar or lemon juice and use as required.

174 GARLIC DRESSING

One of my favourites for all green and mixed salads. If you can't wait overnight for the flavour of the garlic to develop in the dressing, make up the recipe for Classic French Dressing or Vinaigrette Dressing (see Recipes 171 and 172) and substitute garlic salt for ordinary salt.

Cooking time nil

3—4 tablespoons olive oil (or other oil to taste)

$\frac{1}{4}$ level teaspoon salt

$\frac{1}{4}$ level teaspoon dry mustard or $\frac{1}{2}$ level teaspoon Continental

$\frac{1}{2}$ level teaspoon castor sugar or 1 coffee spoon golden syrup

2—3 drops Worcestershire sauce

$\frac{1}{4}$ level teaspoon paprika

$1\frac{1}{2}$—2 level tablespoons wine or cider vinegar or lemon juice

1 halved garlic clove (large or small, depending on taste)

Put oil, salt, mustard, sugar or syrup, Worcestershire sauce and paprika into a basin. Beat until well mixed. Gradually beat in vinegar or lemon juice then pour into a jar or bottle. Add garlic. Cover jar tightly and leave for 12—24 hours. Remove garlic and use dressing as required.

175 HORSERADISH DRESSING

Very good with beef and tongue salads and for side salads served with hot roast beef and beef grills.

Cooking time nil

3—4 tablespoons olive oil (or other oil to taste)
¼ level teaspoon salt
pinch of cayenne pepper
½ level teaspoon castor sugar or 1 coffee spoon golden syrup

1½—2 tablespoons wine or cider vinegar or lemon juice
1—3 level dessertspoons grated horseradish (depending on taste)

Put oil, salt, pepper and sugar or syrup into a basin and beat until well mixed. Gradually beat in vinegar or lemon juice. Finally, stir in horseradish and use as required.

176 PARMESAN CHEESE DRESSING

A subtle dressing for all mixed and green salads, tomato and egg salads and for side salads served with pasta dishes.

Cooking time nil

3—4 tablespoons olive oil (or other oil to taste)
¼ level teaspoon salt
a good shake of white pepper
½ level teaspoon castor sugar or 1 coffee spoon golden syrup
½ level teaspoon Continental mustard

1½—2 tablespoons wine or cider vinegar or lemon juice
3—4 level dessertspoons finely grated Parmesan cheese

Put oil, salt, pepper, sugar or golden syrup and mustard into a basin and beat until well mixed. Gradually beat in vinegar or lemon juice. Finally stir in Parmesan cheese and use as required.

177 RAVIGOTE DRESSING

A piquant dressing (and a classic variation of the Vinaigrette) flavoured with onion, egg, capers, parsley and other fresh herbs. It can be used for all salads and especially with cold roast meat and canned fish.

Cooking time nil

3—4 tablespoons olive oil (or other oil to taste)

a good shake of salt and pepper

$\frac{1}{4}$ level teaspoon dry mustard or $\frac{1}{2}$ level teaspoon Continental

$\frac{1}{2}$ level teaspoon castor sugar or 1 coffee spoon golden syrup

$1\frac{1}{2}$ to 2 tablespoons wine or cider vinegar or lemon juice

1 level tablespoon finely chopped onion

1 finely chopped hard-boiled egg

2 level teaspoons drained and chopped capers

1 level tablespoon very finely chopped parsley

$\frac{1}{2}$ level teaspoon finely chopped fresh tarragon

$\frac{1}{2}$ level teaspoon finely chopped fresh chervil

Put oil, salt, pepper, mustard and sugar or syrup into a basin and beat until well mixed. Gradually beat in vinegar or lemon juice then stir in all remaining ingredients. Use as required.

178 SALSA VERDE (GREEN DRESSING)

An Italian dressing, well flavoured with herbs, capers, parsley, anchovies and garlic and suitable for all green and mixed salads and salads with meat or fish.

153

Cooking time nil

3—4 tablespoons olive oil (or other oil to taste)

a good shake of pepper

½ level teaspoon castor sugar or 1 coffee spoon golden syrup

1½—2 tablespoons lemon juice

1 small garlic clove, very finely chopped

4 anchovy fillets, very finely chopped

3 heaped tablespoons very finely chopped parsley

1 level tablespoon drained and chopped capers

Put oil, pepper and sugar or syrup into a basin and beat until well mixed. Gradually beat in lemon juice then stir in all remaining ingredients. Use as required.

179 SOURED CREAM DRESSING

A deliciously creamy and light dressing that makes a pleasant substitute for mayonnaise. It is particularly good for potato and Russian salads and can also be spooned over hard-boiled eggs, canned fish, cold meats of all descriptions and poultry. And it can be flavoured according to taste. Try adding a tablespoon of chopped chives or parsley or 1 or 2 tablespoons finely chopped fresh celery, or 1 or 2 tablespoons finely grated cucumber, or beat in a tablespoon of tomato purée and a little grated lemon peel. I sometimes add 1 or 2 tablespoons finely chopped pineapple, a teaspoon of grated onion and a shake of paprika.

Cooking time nil

¼ pint carton soured cream

½ level teaspoon castor sugar or 1 coffee spoon golden syrup

¼ level teaspoon salt

a good shake of white pepper

¼ level teaspoon paprika

3 dessertspoons lemon juice or wine vinegar

2—3 tablespoons cream

⅛ teaspoon garlic or onion salt (optional)

Put the soured cream into a basin and beat in the sugar or syrup, salt, pepper and paprika. Gradually beat in lemon juice or vinegar then thin down to taste with cream. Season with garlic or onion salt (if used) and chill lightly before using. If the dressing is still too thick for your personal needs and taste, thin it down further with a little extra cream.

180 LOW CALORIE DRESSING

Specially for dieters. It is oil-free, brightly flavoured and sweetened with sugar substitute and it should please all those who have to eat salads but can't bear them undressed!

Cooking time nil

3 level tablespoons instant non-fat milk granules
3 dessertspoons cold water
3—4 tablespoons fresh lemon juice
1 tablespoon tomato ketchup
$\frac{1}{2}$ teaspoon chilli or Worcestershire sauce
$\frac{1}{2}$ level teaspoon made mustard
a good shake of garlic salt
1 level tablespoon finely chopped parsley
1 level tablespoon finely chopped chives (optional)
powdered sugar substitute to taste

Mix milk granules to a smooth liquid with water. Transfer to a screw-topped jar and add all remaining ingredients, except sugar substitute. Shake briskly until well mixed. Sweeten to taste with sugar substitute and use as required.

181 COOKED SALAD DRESSING

A non-classic dressing that I find extremely useful for all sorts of salads. It is one of those easy dressings

I make when I've run out of oil for mayonnaise or when French or Vinaigrette dressing isn't exactly right. It has an extremely good flavour and is very economical, especially if you need a lot of dressing for a party buffet. I give below the basic recipe.

Once the dressing is made and has cooled down you can pep it up with all sorts of additions; chopped anchovy fillets plus chopped stuffed olives for cold hard-boiled eggs or fish; chopped chives or onion for potato salad; 1 or 2 teaspoons curry powder for a rice salad; a teaspoon of finely grated lemon peel and a tablespoon of chopped walnuts for poultry; 1 or 2 tablespoons finely chopped watercress for salmon and so on. It is the sort of dressing you can do what you like with and it is well behaved. It won't become temperamental and it won't separate out on standing. Three warnings. It does form a skin, so make sure you remove it before using the dressing; it does thicken up a little as it cools, so if it gets too thick for your needs, thin it down with some extra cream or top of milk. Lastly, do not keep it for too long; about 24 hours — covered and in the refrigerator — at the most.

Cooking time 7—10 minutes   *Serves* 8

1 level teaspoon dry mustard
3 level dessertspoons flour
1 level tablespoon castor sugar
$\frac{1}{2}$ level teaspoon salt
2 tablespoons wine or cider vinegar

1 tablespoon lemon juice
$\frac{1}{4}$ pint water
1 large egg
2 tablespoons thin cream
cayenne pepper
onion salt

Put the mustard, flour, sugar and salt into a basin. Gradually mix to a smooth, thin paste with the vinegar, lemon juice and water. Beat egg and add to basin. Stand over a saucepan of gently simmering water;

it should not be boiling too vigorously. Using a hand whisk, gently whisk the dressing until it cooks and thickens and becomes the consistency of whipped cream. Remove from heat and continue whisking until the dressing is smooth. Beat in cream. Add cayenne pepper and onion salt to taste. Cool completely before using. If you know you are going to need a lot of dressing, make up double or even treble the amount given above. If only a little is required, halve all ingredients; instead of the $\frac{1}{4}$ pint water, use 4 table-spoons and a small egg instead of a large one.

The colour of the dressing isn't very exciting. To give it a rich look, beat in a few drops of yellow food colouring.

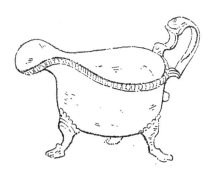

Sweet Sauces

There are no classic sweet sauces in the way there are savoury ones, primarily because many of the classic desserts, puddings or sweets — call them what you will — are complete within themselves and either have the sauce built into them or don't have one at all. There is of course the famous Sauce Melba, Crêpes Suzette Sauce and Crème Chantilly, but even these don't fall into any particular category like, for example, the Béchamel and Espagnole.

Probably our most traditional sauces are the white ones, flavoured according to taste and served with an assortment of pies, tarts and puddings; and rum or brandy butter which we keep for the Christmas plum pudding. And of course, custard sauce.

CUSTARD SAUCE

Custards go back far in history and are described in the Encyclopedia of Practical Cookery, as being 'essentially English preparations, made chiefly of eggs,

sugar and milk mixed together in various proportions...
In France they were at one time known only as
Crèmes à l'Anglaise.'

In the reign of Queen Elizabeth I, the court jesters
of the day went in for their own brand of cabaret
slapstick, which meant they had to leap into an
enormous bowl of custard in front of an audience of
diners. This curious form of amusement caused a good
deal of mirth and it seems obvious now where all the
custard pie humour originated!

In the 16th century, custards — made with cream,
egg yolks, dried fruit but no sugar — were baked in
'coffyns' (another name for pastry cases) a custom
which has lasted right through to the 20th century in
the shape of our modern custard pies and tarts. The
true, traditional custard sauce, made with milk and
thickened with eggs, is a superb and deliciously
flavoured sauce if carefully cooked and, in addition,
is rich in protein and very nourishing. We are all
inclined to make custard these days with milk and
custard powder because it is easy, quick, reliable and
good to eat. But sometimes, for special occasions and
to evoke memories of childhood, the 'old-fashioned'
one is worth remembering even though it is a little
harder to make.

The one danger of an egg-thickened custard is that
it can curdle and separate out into curds and whey
if it is cooked too quickly, cooked over too fierce
a heat or allowed to boil. Consequently it should be
made either in the top of a double saucepan or in
a basin standing over gently simmering—but never
boiling — water andcooled down as quickly as possible
after it has thickened. The sauce may be served warm
or cold and goes well with fruit pies, tarts and flans,
steamed or baked puddings, stewed, canned or fresh
fruit and on top of trifles.

182 CUSTARD SAUCE

Cooking time about 7—9 minutes   *Serves* 4—6

2 standard eggs or 3 egg yolks

1 level tablespoon castor sugar

$\frac{1}{2}$ pint milk

$\frac{1}{4}$—$\frac{1}{2}$ teaspoon vanilla essence

Put the eggs or egg yolks and sugar into a bowl or basin and beat well. Bring milk just up to the boil and whisk into the egg mixture. Strain into the top of a double saucepan or into a basin standing over a saucepan of gently simmering, but not boiling, water. Cook, stirring continuously, until the custard thickens sufficiently to coat the back of the spoon, but do not allow to boil. Remove custard from the heat, stir in essence and pour immediately into a cold jug.

183 CHOCOLATE CUSTARD SAUCE

A sumptuous and rich sauce which can be used to top a rum or sherry trifle or served with any baked or steamed pudding.

Cooking time about 7—9 minutes   *Serves* 6

2 standard eggs or 3 egg yolks

1 level tablespoon castor sugar

$\frac{1}{2}$ pint single cream

2 oz. plain chocolate, chopped or grated (or use chocolate dots)

$\frac{1}{4}$—$\frac{1}{2}$ teaspoon vanilla essence

Put the eggs or egg yolks and sugar into a bowl or basin and beat well. Put cream and chocolate into a saucepan and cook over a low heat, stirring continuously, until the chocolate melts. Bring to the boil then whisk into the egg mixture. Strain into the top of a double saucepan or into a basin standing over a saucepan of gently simmering, but not boiling, water. Cook, stirring all the time, until the custard thickens sufficiently to coat the back of the spoon but do not allow to boil. Remove custard from the heat, stir in the vanilla essence and pour immediately into a cold jug or basin which will prevent the custard from cooking any further. Use as required.

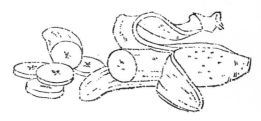

184 COFFEE CUSTARD SAUCE

Delicious with sliced bananas and over steamed or baked chocolate sponge puddings. The sauce, like the chocolate one, may be made with all cream or all milk; it all depends on how extravagant you're feeling!

Cooking time 7—9 minutes *Serves* 4—6

2 standard eggs or 3 egg yolks

1 level tablespoon castor sugar

½ pint milk or single cream

2—3 level teaspoons instant coffee powder

Put the eggs or egg yolks and sugar into a bowl or basin and beat well. Put milk or cream into a saucepan. Add coffee and slowly bring to the boil. Whisk into the egg mixture and strain into the top of a double saucepan or into a basin standing over a saucepan of gently simmering, but not boiling, water. Cook, stirring continuously, until the custard thickens

161

sufficiently to coat the back of the spoon, but do not allow to boil. Remove the custard from the heat and pour immediately into a cold jug or basin which will prevent the custard from cooking any further. Use as required.

185 LEMON OR ORANGE CUSTARD

Light, refreshing and fragrant — a perfect sauce for fruity sweets.

Cooking time 7—9 minutes *Serves* 4—6

½ pint milk
a strip of lemon or orange peel, 4 inches long
2 standard eggs or 3 egg yolks

1 level tablespoon castor sugar

Pour the milk into a saucepan. Add the lemon or orange peel and bring to the boil. Remove from heat and leave to stand for 5 minutes so that the flavour of the lemon or orange peel penetrates the milk. Beat eggs or egg yolks and sugar well together. Whisk in the milk then strain into the top of a double saucepan or into a basin standing over a saucepan of gently simmering, but not boiling, water. Cook, stirring all the time, until the custard thickens sufficiently to coat the back of the spoon, but do not allow to boil. Remove the custard from the heat and pour immediately into a cold jug or basin which will prevent the custard from cooking any further. Use as required.

186 NUT CUSTARD

This recipe comes from a book published in 1893, called 'Novel Dishes for Vegetarian Households', written by Mary Pope. It sounds rather delicious and certainly makes a change from other custard sauce recipes. 'Nearly all the nuts amalgamate well with custard and form an agreeable variety. The nuts should be ground in the mill and simmered with the milk for 10 minutes before the eggs are stirred in. Almonds and pistachios are the best for this purpose. Blanch them before grinding — fewer eggs are required than for plain custard. A little cream is an improvement. Chestnuts should be boiled before being ground.' No mention is made of sugar but I would add 1 level tablespoon of castor sugar.

187 CUSTARD POWDER SAUCE

The all-round family favourite and a sauce which I make differently from the accepted and conventional methods laid down on packets, tins and in books. Why? Only because it's easier and gives me one less utensil to wash up!

Cooking time 5—6 minutes *Serves* 4

3 level dessertspoons custard powder (use 1 extra dessertspoon for a thicker custard)

½ pint milk
2—3 level dessertspoons granulated sugar

Put custard powder into a saucepan. Using a wooden spoon, mix it to a thin, smooth cream with some of the cold milk. Pour in rest of milk and mix well. Stand the saucepan over a low heat and cook, stirring continuously, until the custard comes to the boil and thickens. Simmer for 1 minute, remove from heat and stir in sugar to taste.

I add the sugar after the custard has boiled because it reduces the risk of burning. Serve the custard hot or cold, according to taste.

SWEET WHITE SAUCES

White sauces which are served with desserts are exactly the same, apart from the addition of sugar, as the savoury white sauces made by the blending and roux methods described earlier on in the book. (See pages 8 to 13.) As a general rule the sauces should be of a coating consistency, but a slightly thinner sauce may be made if preferred. I proceed in the same manner as if I were making a savoury sauce, minus pepper and salt, and only when the sauce comes to the boil and has thickened and simmered for the required amount of time, do I add the sugar. I find if it is added earlier on the sauce is more inclined to stick and burn across the base of the saucepan. The sauce may be served entirely without additions or may be flavoured to taste. Personally, I find a sweet white sauce a bit on the negative side unless it's got something added and consequently my two basic recipes contain vanilla essence which you may include if you want to or omit if you don't.

188 VANILLA SAUCE 1 (BLENDING METHOD)

Suitable for baked or steamed puddings, fruit pies, tarts and turnovers and stewed, canned or fresh fruit.

Cooking time 7—9 minutes *Serves* 4

1 oz. (2 level tablespoons) cornflour
½ pint cold milk
2—3 level dessertspoons granulated sugar

a small knob or 1 teaspoon butter or margarine
¼—½ teaspoon vanilla essence

Blend cornflour to a smooth cream with a little of the cold milk. Pour rest of milk into a saucepan and bring up to the boil. Pour on to cornflour cream, stirring briskly all the time. Return to saucepan. Cook over a low heat until sauce comes to the boil and thickens, stirring or whisking continuously with a wooden spoon, light balloon whisk or other hand whisk to prevent lumps from forming. Add sugar, butter or margarine and vanilla essence and simmer very gently, stirring, for 3 minutes or until the sugar has dissolved. Serve straight away.

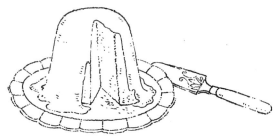

189 VANILLA SAUCE 2 (ROUX METHOD)

Cooking time 7—9 minutes *Serves 4*

1 oz. butter or margarine
1 oz. (2 level tablespoons) flour
$\frac{1}{2}$ pint cold milk

2—3 level dessertspoons granulated sugar
$\frac{1}{4}$—$\frac{1}{2}$ teaspoon vanilla essence

Melt the butter or margarine in a heavy-based saucepan. When foamy, stir in flour. Cook slowly for 3 minutes, stirring all the time (on no account allow the roux to brown). Remove from heat. Gradually add the milk, beating well after each addition (or add all the milk in one go). When sauce is smooth, return to heat. Cook, stirring with a wooden spoon all the time (or whisking with a hand whisk, depending on the method you've chosen, see page 9) until the sauce comes to the boil and thickens. Add sugar and vanilla essence and simmer very gently, stirring, for 3 minutes or until the sugar has dissolved. Serve straight away.

190 BRANDY OR RUM SAUCE

A popular one for Christmas pudding and mince pies. Instead of brandy or rum, sweet sherry may be added if preferred or even whisky, as an interesting change.

Make up the Vanilla Sauce recipe 1 or 2 (see Recipes 188 and 189) but omit the vanilla essence. After the sauce has come to the boil and thickened, add 1 or 2 tablespoons brandy, rum, sherry or whisky with all the remaining ingredients.

191 CHOCOLATE SAUCE 1
(COCOA POWDER)

It was Montezuma, a Mexican king, who appears to have created the very first chocolate sauce. Round about 1520, he mixed cocoa and water with thick cream and vanilla and served it to his guests from a golden bowl with a golden ladle. It is not clear what was done with this exotic brew, but one assumes it was drunk and not, at that time, served as a sauce.

This chocolate sauce is not the dark and rich one usually reserved for ice cream and ice cream sundaes, but a simple white sauce flavoured with cocoa and vanilla essence. It can be served with any steamed or baked pudding, especially those made with chocolate, ginger, coffee or dried fruit such as raisins or dates.

Cooking time 7—9 minutes   *Serves* 4

1 level tablespoon cocoa powder	3—4 level dessertspoons granulated sugar
1 level tablespoon cornflour	½—1 teaspoon vanilla essence
½ pint cold milk	¼—½ oz. butter or margarine

Blend the cocoa powder and cornflour to a smooth cream with a little of the cold milk. Pour rest of milk into a saucepan and bring to the boil. Pour on to cocoa and cornflour cream, stirring briskly all the time. Return to saucepan. Cook over a low heat until sauce comes to the boil and thickens, stirring continuously with a wooden spoon or whisking gently with a light balloon whisk or hand whisk. Add sugar, vanilla essence and butter or margarine and simmer very gently, stirring, for 3 minutes, or until the sugar has dissolved. Serve straight away.

192 CHOCOLATE SAUCE 2 (PLAIN CHOCOLATE)

This is a slightly richer sauce than the cocoa powder one in that it is made with block chocolate. It, too, can be served with all types of steamed and baked puddings.

Cooking time 10—12 minutes   *Serves* 4—6

½ pint cold milk	1 oz. flour
2 oz. plain chocolate, chopped, or chocolate dots	½—1 teaspoon vanilla essence
1 oz. butter or margarine	2—3 level dessertspoons granulated sugar

Put milk and chocolate into a saucepan and stand over a low heat until chocolate has completely melted. Leave until almost cold. Melt the butter or margarine in a heavy-based saucepan. When foamy, stir in flour. Cook slowly for 3 minutes, stirring all the time (on no account allow the roux to brown). Remove from heat. Gradually add the chocolate and milk mixture, beating well after each addition (or add all the liquid in one go). When sauce is smooth, return to heat. Cook, stirring with a wooden spoon all the time (or whisking with a hand whisk, depending on the method you've chosen, see page 9) until the sauce comes to the boil and thickens. Add vanilla essence and sugar and simmer very gently, stirring, for 3 minutes or until the sugar has dissolved then serve.

HARD BUTTER SAUCES

In North America these are always referred to as hard sauces — while over here we know them better as Brandy or Rum Butters. Hard sauce is probably the most apt description since by the time it is served, the sauce should be quite firm and the consistency of chilled butter cream.

The Butters, or Hard Sauces, are traditionally used to accompany the Christmas pudding or any other rich and fruity steamed or boiled puddings, and are considered to be rich and luxurious concoctions and to some extent an acquired taste. They should always be made with fresh, unsalted butter and either castor or soft brown sugar; the slight crunchiness coming from the sugar gives these sauces their characteristic texture, which is why a powder sugar such as icing is not, as a rule, recommended in cookery books. However, if you prefer, as I do, a smoother sauce, use half icing sugar with half castor or soft brown sugar.

193 BRANDY BUTTER (OR BRANDY HARD SAUCE)

Serves 6—8

4 oz. unsalted, softened
  butter
4 oz. castor sugar (or use
  half castor and half
  sifted icing sugar)
2 tablespoons brandy
1 oz. ground almonds
  (optional)
mixed spice

Put the butter into a bowl and beat until light.
Gradually beat in the sugar (or mixture of sugars)
alternately with the brandy. Continue beating until
the mixture is light and fluffy. Stir in almonds (if used)
then either pipe or spoon the butter into a small
serving dish. Chill until firm and sprinkle the top
lightly with spice before serving.

194 RUM BUTTER (OR RUM HARD SAUCE)

Serves 6—8

4 oz. unsalted, softened
  butter
4 oz. soft brown sugar
  (or use half brown and
  half sifted icing sugar)
2 tablespoons rum
1 oz. ground almonds
  (optional)
$\frac{1}{2}$ level teaspoon finely grated
  lemon peel
cinnamon

Put the butter into a bowl and beat until light.
Gradually beat in the sugar (or mixture of sugars)
alternately with the rum. Continue beating until the
mixture is light and fluffy. Stir in almonds (if used)
and the lemon peel. Either spoon or pipe the butter
into a small serving dish. Chill until firm and sprinkle
the top lightly with cinnamon before serving.

195 WHISKY BUTTER (OR WHISKY HARD SAUCE)

This is one of my own adaptations of the basic recipe. I use whisky instead of brandy or rum and flavour the sauce with walnuts and orange peel. It has a most beautiful, subtle flavour and is heavenly spread thickly over hot, wafer-thin pancakes. The walnuts should be ground, either in a blender or coffee mill. If you haven't either, chop the nuts as finely as you can.

Serves 6—8

4 oz. unsalted, softened butter	2 tablespoons whisky
4 oz. castor sugar (or use half castor and half sifted icing sugar)	1 oz. ground walnuts
	$\frac{1}{2}$—1 level teaspoon finely grated orange peel
	nutmeg

Put the butter into a bowl and beat until light. Gradually beat in the sugar (or mixture of sugars) alternately with the whisky. Continue beating until the mixture is light and fluffy. Stir in the walnuts and orange peel and then either pipe or spoon the butter into a small serving dish. Chill until firm and sprinkle the top lightly with nutmeg before serving.

MISCELLANEOUS SWEET SAUCES

196 CRÈME CHANTILLY

This is one of those elegant and sophisticated classic sauces or toppings that is simple to make and versatile; it can be served with almost any hot or cold dessert and is less rich and goes further than ordinary double cream. It can be flavoured to taste with either vanilla essence or finely grated lemon or orange peel.

Serves 6—8

¼ pint double cream, lightly
  chilled
4 tablespoons single cream,
  lightly chilled
2 level tablespoons sifted
  icing sugar

¼ teaspoon vanilla essence or
  ¼ level teaspoon finely
  grated lemon or orange
  peel
1 egg white

Put both creams into a cold bowl and whisk until *just*
thick. Do not overwhip or the cream may become
buttery. Gently stir in sugar and essence or lemon or
orange peel. Beat egg white to a stiff snow. Fold into
cream mixture with a large metal spoon and serve
straight away.

197 ORANGE FLOWER WATER SAUCE

Mrs. Agnes B. Marshall, whose recipe this is, lived
during the nineteenth century, and, apart from being
very beautiful and an able and talented cook, she had
an extremely good head for business! She wrote
books — 'Mrs. A. B. Marshall's Cookery Book' was
one of them — ran a cookery school in central London
which was 'the largest and most successful of its
kind' and had her own brand of essences, spices,
icing sugar and canned hors d'oeuvre which she
displayed and sold, along with an enormous range of
kitchen utensils, at the school.

The Orange Flower Water Sauce is one I had never
come across before, so I tested it (using half quantities
and a double saucepan) and found it delicate and
charming. Orange flower water smells faintly of eau
de Cologne and is available from most chemists at
a fairly reasonable price. Make it if you like a faintly
perfumed sauce and serve it, as Mrs. Marshall suggest-
ed, with hot or cold soufflés and puddings. *Half the
amount given below should be sufficient for 6.*

'Put into a stew pan (*I used the top of a double saucepan*) 8 large yolks of eggs, 3 tablespoons orange flower water, 3 oz. castor sugar, 3 tablespoons thick cream and a saltspoonful of essence of vanilla. Stir these all together until it comes to the thickness of cream, standing the stew pan in a *bain marie;* when thick, rub it through a tammy. It may be poured round the sweet and sprinkled with crystallised rose leaves, or served in a boat with the leaves lightly sprinkled on top.'

198 CRÊPES SUZETTE SAUCE

Legend has it that Crêpes Suzette was created for a French actress of the same name by an appreciative but anonymous chef. Be that as it may, the dish itself, which includes a rich and flamboyant sauce, has international appeal and every big restaurant in every big city seems to have Crêpes Suzette as a speciality on its menu. For those who want to try it in the seclusion of their own homes, here is the classic recipe. If you think I've been a bit frugal with the alcohol, add more liqueur by all means, but go easy on the brandy; too much and you'll lose the fragrant and subtle flavour of the orange. Because the sauce is not usually served on its own, I have included pancakes in the list of ingredients.

Cooking time 10—12 minutes *Serves* 4

3 oz. unsalted butter	juice of 1 medium orange
2 oz. sifted icing sugar	2—3 tablespoons Cointreau
¼ level teaspoon finely grated lemon peel	or Grand Marnier
	8 cooked pancakes (*crêpes*)
½ level teaspoon finely grated orange peel	2 tablespoons brandy

Melt the butter in a large frying pan. Add the sugar, lemon and orange peel, orange juice and the Cointreau or Grand Marnier. Heat through slowly for 5 minutes. Meanwhile, fold the pancakes in half and then in half again. Add to the pan. Heat for 4 minutes, turning twice and basting frequently with sauce. Just before serving, warm the brandy, pour it quickly over the pancakes and set light to it with a match. Serve as soon as the flames have died down.

If you are wondering why the brandy has to be warmed first, it's because it burns more successfully.

199 MELBA SAUCE

Peach or Pêche, Melba is seen on menus even more frequently than Crêpes Suzette, and one wonders how many people realise that it, too, was invented by one of the great chefs in honour of a famous nineteenth-century opera singer. The chef in question was Escoffier, and the lady, Dame Nellie Melba. When this dish was originally created (during the late 1800's while Escoffier was still at the Savoy Hotel) it consisted of a bed of vanilla ice cream, topped with peaches and decorated with an iced swan. Some time afterwards, when Escoffier moved to the Carlton in London, he added the finishing touches by poaching the peaches in a vanilla-flavoured syrup and then masking the fruit with a raspberry sauce. A true and faithful Pêche Melba should be made with fresh ripe peaches and fresh raspberries. All too often we get a compromise; indifferent ice cream, canned peaches and a sticky, jammy sauce that obviously bears little resemblance to the original. I give below a very simple recipe for the Melba—or raspberry—sauce, using fresh fruit and little else. Escoffier didn't, I believe, use raspberry jam or redcurrant jelly; nor have I.

Cooking time 2—3 minutes *Serves* 4

12 oz. fresh raspberries | 2 teaspoons cold water
1½ level teaspoons arrowroot | sifted icing sugar to taste
| red food colouring

Rub the raspberries through the finest possible nylon sieve. Transfer the purée to a saucepan. Mix the arrowroot to a smooth cream with the cold water. Add to pan. Cook over a medium heat, stirring all the time, until the raspberry purée comes to the boil. As soon as it has thickened and cleared, remove the pan from the heat. Sweeten to taste with icing sugar then add a few drops of red food colouring to heighten the colour. Pour into a bowl and leave until completely cold before using.

200 JAM SAUCE

An old favourite for boiled or steamed sponge and baked puddings. The jam can be any one you fancy: the three nicest are raspberry, strawberry and black-currant.

Cooking time 6—7 minutes *Serves* 4—6

6 level tablespoons jam	1—2 level tablespoons castor
2 level teaspoons arrowroot	sugar
¼ pint cold water	1 or 2 teaspoons lemon juice

Put the jam into a heavy-based saucepan and stand over a low heat. Mix the arrowroot to a smooth cream with some of the cold water. Gradually stir in rest of water. Add to jam in the saucepan and increase heat to medium. Cook, stirring all the time, until the sauce comes to the boil. As soon as it has thickened and cleared, remove from heat and stir in sugar and lemon juice. Serve hot.

201 MARMALADE SAUCE

Another popular sauce for baked, steamed and boiled puddings. I like it made with chunky marmalade, so that one gets those delicious chewy pieces of orange peel. If you prefer a smooth sauce with no bits, use a jellied marmalade.

Make in exactly the same way as the Jam Sauce (see Recipe 200), but use marmalade instead of jam.

202 SYRUP SAUCE (1)

The perfect sauce for all sorts of hot puddings. In case some of you have difficulty in getting the syrup out of its container, here is one way which works very well for me. Dip the spoon (which should be a metal one) in very hot or boiling water before dipping it into the can or jar of syrup. The heat of the spoon will melt the syrup slightly and it will then come out of the can or jar and off the spoon quite easily.

Cooking time 5—7 minutes *Serves* 4

6 level tablespoons golden syrup
2 tablespoons hot water
½ level teaspoon finely grated lemon or orange peel (optional)
juice of ½ a lemon

Put all the ingredients into a saucepan and heat through gently, stirring all the time. Serve hot.

203 SYRUP SAUCE (2)

For those who prefer a less sweet and more diluted sauce, the recipe below may be more suitable.

Cooking time 5—7 minutes *Serves* 4—6

6 level tablespoons golden syrup
2 level teaspoons arrowroot
6 tablespoons cold water
finely grated peel and juice of ½ a medium lemon

Put the syrup into a thick-based saucepan and stand over a low heat. Mix the arrowroot to a smooth cream with some of the cold water. Stir in rest of water. Add to syrup in the saucepan with the lemon peel and juice. Cook, stirring all the time, until the sauce comes to the boil. As soon as it has thickened and cleared, remove from heat and serve straight away.

204 FRUIT SYRUP SAUCE

For the occasions when you open a large can of fruit for a certain dish and then wonder what to do with the syrup that is left over! I have included a tablespoon of sherry which greatly improves the all-round flavour. The sauce is suitable for steamed, baked or boiled puddings and hot sweets prepared with the canned fruit itself.

Cooking time 6—7 minutes *Serves* 4—6

¼ pint fruit syrup
2 level teaspoons arrowroot
3 tablespoons water
1 tablespoon lemon juice

1 tablespoon sweet sherry
yellow, green or red food colouring

Put the syrup into a saucepan. Mix the arrowroot to a smooth cream with some of the water. Gradually stir in rest of water with the lemon juice. Cook, stirring all the time, until the sauce comes to the boil. As soon as it has thickened and cleared, remove from heat. Stir in sherry then tint pale yellow, green or pink with the food colouring. Serve hot.

205 ZABAGLIONE SAUCE

An exquisite sauce from Italy. It can be transferred to warm glasses and served as a sweet with thin, crisp biscuits or it can be used as a sauce for rich fruit puddings and mince pies and tarts. It is delicious served warm with fruit salad or with hot stewed fruits such as apricots. The traditional recipe is made with egg yolks only, but for a lighter and fluffier texture, and to make the sauce go further, one or two beaten egg whites may be folded in at the end.

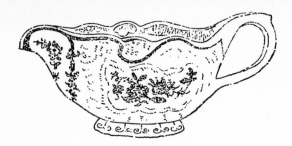

Cooking time about 10 minutes *Serves* 4

4 egg yolks
4 level tablespoons sifted icing sugar

1 sherry glass Marsala
1 or 2 egg whites (optional)

Put the egg yolks and sugar into a basin standing over a saucepan of hot — but not boiling — water, making sure the base of the basin isn't touching the water. Beat with a wire whisk until foamy. Add the Marsala gradually and continue beating until the mixture is light and fluffy and almost double its original bulk. Remove the basin from the saucepan of water and either serve the sauce straight away or fold in stiffly beaten egg white or whites first.

206 WEINSCHAUM SAUCE

A German sauce which means wine foam. The Germans serve it with vanilla pudding which is something like our blancmange. To me this seems a waste; I prefer it with canned or stewed fruits or steamed puddings.

Cooking time 10—15 minutes *Serves* 4

¼ pint (plus 4 tablespoons) dry white wine
1 tablespoon water

2 large eggs
2 oz. castor sugar

178

Put wine, water, unbeaten eggs and sugar into a basin standing over a saucepan of hot, but not boiling, water. Beat continuously with a wire whisk until the sauce thickens and becomes foamy. Do not allow to boil. Serve straight away.

207 SABAYON SAUCE

This is the cold version (the hot one is very similar to Zabaglione sauce) which can be served with rich steamed fruit puddings, fruit salads, fruit flans, pies and tarts and over portions of chocolate cake.

Cooking time about 10 minutes *Serves* 4

2 egg yolks	3 tablespoons dry sherry
3 oz. castor sugar	4 tablespoons double cream
1 tablespoon water	

Put the egg yolks, sugar, water and sherry into a basin standing over a saucepan of hot, but not boiling, water. Beat continuously with a wire whisk until the mixture becomes very thick. Do not allow to boil. Remove basin from the saucepan of water and either stand in iced water or surround with ice cubes. Continue beating until the sauce is cold. Then fold in the cream, whipped until stiff. Chill thoroughly before serving.

208 HOT CHOCOLATE SAUCE

Gorgeous over ice cream and economical to make.

Cooking time about 8 minutes *Serves* 4

3 oz. soft brown sugar	3 dessertspoons cold milk
1 oz. butter	$\frac{1}{2}$ teaspoon vanilla essence
3 level dessertspoons sifted cocoa powder	

Put all the ingredients into a heavy-based saucepan and stir over a low heat until the butter has melted and the sauce is smooth. Bring to the boil and boil steadily for 4 minutes. Serve straight away.

209 MARSHMALLOW FUDGE SAUCE

Another delicious, buttery sauce for serving over ice cream and ice cream sundaes.

Cooking time 7—8 minutes *Serves* 6

4 oz. butter	2 tablespoons single cream
3 oz. soft brown sugar	$\frac{1}{4}$ teaspoon vanilla essence
4 oz. marshmallows	

Put the butter, sugar, marshmallows and cream into a saucepan. Stand over a low heat and stir until the ingredients have melted. Add vanilla essence and slowly bring to the boil, stirring continuously. Boil gently for 5 minutes then serve straight away.

Postscript

From the Encyclopedia of Practical Cookery comes this explanation on gravies which sets out to prove that while unthickened gravy is blue blooded and British, the thickened gravy that we eat today has been 'borrowed' from the French. 'The literal meaning of gravy is the sediment of that which drains from cooked meat; that is, the juices of the meat, which being heavier than the hot fat sink to the bottom...

'The French term for gravy is *jus*, so that meat served *au jus* is served with its own gravy and not with a made sauce. As the inclination of the French cook is generally towards some rectification or elaboration of plain foods, they are very much inclined to operate upon plain gravies; to them it seems as though to serve plain gravy or meat juice with a dish, whether a roasted joint or ragoût, would be desecrating, by neglect, the fine art of cooking; to obviate such a culinary error and yet use that which must be acknowledged to be the legitimate sauce of the meat, its own juices, they have instituted a *jus lié*, which means thickened juice, or gravy combined with something to make it stronger *(such as arrowroot or cornflour)*.

'When it is desired to thicken a gravy, *jus lié*, this can be done by a judicious use of flour, or the addition of some other starchy material; but for all ordinary purposes, as far as bona fide roasted meat is concerned, the plain gravy is mostly preferred upon our English tables.'

The ladle, also known as the hlaedel, ladele, laddil, ladill, ladyl, ladyll, ladell, ladil and ladul, goes back to about 1100 or 1200 B. C. when Roman cooks used them in much the same way as we do today; for lifting bubbling beef and gravy out of a stew pot (or to be more accurate a cauldron!) The basic shape hasn't changed much in all these thousands of years—it remains still a circular bowl on a long handle—but whereas in later years ladles were made from silver and other metals and were fairly simple, the Roman ladles were usually in bronze and were highly ornamental and decorative, as were many of the cooking utensils and eating and drinking vessels of that period.

In Medieval times, ladles became simpler altogether and were made — usually in the home or by a local carpenter — from wood, while much later, in the 17th and 18th centuries, ladles made from silver were quite common. It was during the Victorian era that copper and brass ladles became so popular and since then, of course, ladles have been manufactured from practically every metal imaginable.

The 20th century has brought little change where the ladle is concerned. Despite modernisation of kitchen equipment and kitchen utensils over the years, no one has, as yet, been able to improve on that seemingly anachronistic and timeless style and design developed, so long ago, by those Roman craftsmen, and you can be sure that the ladle, big or small, ornamenting your kitchen wall or sitting in the cutlery drawer is a copy of a very old and treasured museum piece.

Sauce-boats

Sauces were originally served in saucers; shallow dishes made from an assortment of metals. The earliest silver sauce-boat, with the traditional oval body, made its first appearance during the reign of George 1 towards the end of the 17th century. They were fairly complicated affairs with a pouring spout and handle each end. During the middle of the 18th century, the design of sauce-boats changed; some had a pouring lip at one end and a handle at the other, while others had no pouring lip or spout at all, but were covered with lids and looked like small tureens. Later on in the 18th century, when design was greatly influenced by Robert Adam, sauce-boats, which were still lidded, were shaped like elegant urns with a handle at either end. During the 19th century, sauce-boats returned to their earlier shape and once more had a pouring lip at one end and a handle at the other end. Silver enthusiasts and curio collectors should take a look round their lofts and attics! A pair of George I sauce-boats, made in 1726, each with double lips and two spouts, were auctioned recently for £10,000, while a pair made in 1735, during the reign of George II, were auctioned for £6,000.

Saucepans

The Romans, with their sophisticated tastes and highly cultivated palates, had a great fondness for heavily spiced sauces with their poultry, goose and peacocks (among other foods which included thrushes, larks and nightingale tongues!) and had pans — sauce-pans — especially made from bronze for cooking them. The shape was more like a frying pan than the saucepan as we know it today — circular, shallow and with a long handle — and because the pan was placed over an open fire, it was thick and heavy to stand up to the heat.

In the Middle Ages (from about 1066 to 1485) cooking utensils were cruder and less 'modern' in style than in Roman times and the saucepan, still kept for sauces, was made from iron and had three legs tripod fashion and a long handle.

During the Tudor and Stuart periods — the 16th and 17th centuries — there was little change in the shape of cooking utensils although the large cauldron-type pots and shallower skillets with legs, produced during the Middle Ages, were gradually disappearing and being replaced by flat-based pots and pans made from copper, brass and iron. And there was still the saucepan for sauces, but this time it had a curved, ridged handle fixed to both sides of the pan, giving it the appearance of a shallow basket with a carrying handle.

During the 18th and 19th centuries, the term sauce-pan seemed to apply to all pots and pans used for general cooking purposes and the saucepan of the previous centuries became the contemporary frying pan or skillet.

The Victorian Table and the Place of Sauces

The following advice comes from a book called 'The Practical Housewife', which was published about the middle of the last century.

'In arranging or laying out a table, several things require particular attention, and especially the following: — Plate should be well cleaned, and have a bright polish; few things look worse than to see a greasy-looking epergne and streaky spoons. Glass should be well rubbed with a wash leather, dipped in a solution of fine whiting and stone-blue, and then dried; afterwards it should be polished with an old silk handkerchief.

'Plates and dishes should be hot, otherwise the guests will be disgusted by seeing flakes of fat floating about in the gravy. Bread should be cut in pieces about an inch thick, and each round of a loaf into six parts, or if for a dinner party, dinner rolls should be ordered. The bread is placed under the napkins, or on the left of each guest; if dinner napkins are not used, some of the bread being placed in a bread-tray covered with a crochet cloth upon the sideboard.

'Lights, either at or after the dinner, should be subdued, and above the guests, if possible, so as to be shed upon the table, without intercepting the view. Sauces, either bottle, sweet, or boat, vegetables, and sliced cucumber, or glazed onions for stubble goose, should be placed upon the sideboard; a plate basket for removing the soiled plates is usually placed under the sideboard, or some other convenient part of the room; and two knife-trays, covered with napkins, are placed upon a butler's tray; these are used for removing soiled carvers and forks, and the soiled silver. It is useful to have a large-sized bradawl, a corkscrew, and funnel, with strainer; the former to break the wire of the champagne bottles, and the latter to strain port wine, if required to be opened during dinner.'

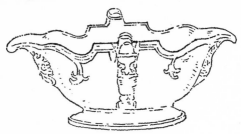

The Romans and Their Sauces

A few words on the subject from the 'Magazine of Domestic Economy' published in 1837.

'When the brush of civilisation had rubbed off the asperities of the ancient Romans, and the once rude, iron-framed, and coarse-mannered soldiers of the republic had, under the emperors, become, like the Athenians in the zenith of their prosperity, the most polished and courteous, as well as the most arrogant, among contemporary nations, the most fastidious improvements and fashions were adopted that good taste, fancy, or caprice, could suggest, and the fashion or mode at any particular season was as absorbing, as tyrannical, and as omnipotent — we may also add sometimes as ridiculous — as we see the fashions of our own metropolis at the present day. The Roman exquisite, seventeen centuries ago, was but a type of the London or Parisian exquisite of 1837.

'As social refinement progresses among any people, there is no one enjoyment of life which elicits more general attention, and requires more care than the art of preparing the food by which we live, — the art of rendering an enjoyment which nature has imposed upon us as a necessity. And we shall always see the subtleties of the culinary art keep pace with the operation of the social polishing wheel.

'Cookery and the luxuries of the table were, therefore, main objects of study to the wealthy of ancient Rome; and both were carried to an excess, and led to an expenditure from which a modern Apicius, even though a millionaire member of the corporation of London, would shrink with dismay. A sum sufficient for a large fortune, in our times, was often given for a single dish that would scarcely suffice to satisfy the cravings of one hungry man, but a mere taste of which was deemed sufficient at the well-spread and luxurious board of the Roman patrician. Epicurism in food was therefore carried, in ancient Rome, quite as far, if not farther, than among the turtle and venison feeders of this metropolis; with only this difference, that the latter are more gross and animalised — not to say more hoggish, — whilst the former were more refined, more elegant, more intellectual, combining with their banquets "the flow of soul" that bursts from poetry and art, and the "feast of reason", enjoyed by a conversation from which flowed a rich and glorious stream of philosophy and knowledge.'

The author then gives a dissertation on Roman cooking, followed by an assortment of recipes for salmon, lobster and eels, and concludes with a selection of ketchups. For amusement only, here are two of them!

'*Oyster Ketchup.* — Bruise two hundred of oysters, and put them, together with their liquor, two pounds of anchovies, two sliced lemons with the peel of one, into three bottles of good white wine. Boil the whole gently during an hour, then strain it through muslin.

Add to the strained liquor, half an ounce of cloves, half an ounce of allspice, some peppercorns, and two nutmegs sliced. Boil this twenty minutes longer, and a little while before you take it off the fire, throw in some salt and twenty-four shallots. Let it have a few boils more. Pour it into a vessel to cool, and when cold, bottle it. This ketchup, if properly corked, and the cork covered with bladder and sealed, will keep good for years.

'*Anchovy Ketchup*. — Into two gallons of very stale ale, the stronger the better, put a pound and half of anchovies washed and cleansed from the entrails, half an ounce of mace, the same quantity of cloves, a quarter of an ounce of allspice, the same quantity of long pepper, four chilies, half a dozen lumps of ginger, a pound of shalots, six lumps of sugar, and two quarts and a half of large mushrooms, well rubbed and picked. Boil all this slowly in a well-tinned stewpan, during an hour; then run the liquor through a jelly bag. Let it stand until cold, then bottle it, cork the bottles well, tie a bit of bladder over each cork, and cover the bladder with sealing wax. This is the most delicious of fish sauces, and one tablespoon of it will suffice for a pin of melted butter. This ketchup will keep good more than twenty years.'

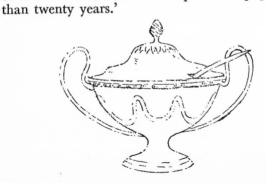

INDEX

Aïoli sauce 66
Allemande sauce 30
Álmond butter sauce 80
Amandine butter 84
Anchovy butter 84
Anchovy sauce 13
Anchovy sauce (Italian) 101
Andalouse sauce 67
Apple sauce 107
Apple sauce (brown) 108
Apple sauce with cider 107
Aurore sauce 25
Avocado mayonnaise 64

Bacon marinade 124
Bagna cauda 102
Barbecue sauce for pork, duck and goose 92
Barbecue sauces 91—4
Bavaroise sauce 53
Béarnaise sauce 53
Béchamel sauce 19
Bercy butter 85
Bercy sauce 108
Beurre manié 109
Beurre noisette 78
Beurres composés 82—90
Bigarade (or orange) sauce 45
Black butter sauce 78
Black butter sauce with capers 79
Blender mayonnaise 64
Blue cheese dressing 150
Bolognese sauce 97
Bordelaise sauce 39
Bourguignonne sauce 111
Brandy butter (or brandy hard sauce) 169
Brandy sauce 166
Bread sauce 110—11
Brown butter sauce 78
Brown sauces 32—45

Burgundy sauce 111
Butter crumb sauce 80
Butter sauces 76—81. *See also* Beurres composés, Hard butter sauces

Caboul sauce 67
Camp ketchup 139
Caper sauce 13
Caviare butter 85
Celery sauce 29
Celery sauce for fish 143
Chantilly mayonnaise 68
Charcutière sauce 42
Chasseur sauce 40
Chaud-froid sauce 20
Cheese and mushroom sauce for macaroni 143
Cheese sauce 14
Chestnut sauce 112
Chicken and almond sauce 144
Chive butter 86
Chive sauce 131
Chocolate custard sauce 160
Chocolate sauce (cocoa powder) 166
Chocolate sauce (hot) 179
Chocolate sauce (plain chocolate) 167
Choron sauce 54
Cider barbecue sauce 94
Cider marinade 127
Coating sauce 9
Coating sauce — roux method 12
Cocktail sauce 68
Coffee custard sauce 161
Colbert butter 86
Cooked salad dressing 155—7
Cranberry and apple sauce 115
Cranberry sauce 113—15
Crème Chantilly 170

Creole sauce 115
Creole—style sauce, quick 144
Crêpes Suzette sauce 172
Cucumber sauce (Doria sauce) 21
Cucumber sauce (mayonnaise) 69
Cumberland sauce (cold) 118
Cumberland sauce (hot) 116
Currant sauce for venison or pork 118
Curry butter 87
Curry sauce 119
Custard powder sauce 163
Custard sauces 158—63

Demi-glace sauce 44
Devil butter 87
Diane sauce 43
Doria or cucumber sauce 21
Dressings see salad dressings
Dutch sauce 22

Egg-based sauces 46—75
Egg and lemon sauce 134
Egg sauce 14
Epicurienne sauce 69
Espagnole (or brown) sauce 38
Estragon sauce 26

Flamande sauce 31
Foyot sauce 54
French dressing (classic) 149
French dressing (Vinaigrette) 150
Fruit syrup sauce 177

Game marinade, Victorian 127
Garlic butter 87
Garlic dressing 151
Garlic mayonnaise 66
Garlic sauce 104
Gooseberry sauce 120
Gravies 121
Green butter 88

Green dressing 153
Green mayonnaise (sauce verte) 69
Grill sauce 121
Guaymas sauce 70

Hard butter sauces 168—70
Hollandaise sauce 46—52
Horseradish butter 89
Horseradish dressing 152
Horseradish relish 122
Horseradish sauce (hot) 21
Hot sauce 140
Hungarian butter (Paprika butter) 90
Hungarian sauce 26
Hunters' sauce (Chasseur sauce) 40

Italian mayonnaise 105
Italian sauces 95—105

Jam sauce 175

Lemon butter sauce 79
Lemon custard 162
Lemon sauce 15
Liver sauce 100
Louis sauce 70
Low calorie dressing 155
Lyonnaise sauce 42

Madeira sauce 45
Maître d'hôtel butter 89
Maître d'hôtel sauce 15
Maltese sauce 54
Marchand de vin sauce 40
Marinades 123—7
Marmalade sauce 175
Marshmallow fudge sauce 180
Maximilian sauce 71
Mayonnaise and mayonnaise-based sauces 56—75, 105
Meat sauce 98
Medici sauce 55

Melba sauce 174
Meunière (or lemon) butter sauce 79
Mint sauce 128
Mock Hollandaise sauce 22
Mornay sauce 22
Mousquetaire (or Musketeer) sauce 72
Mousseline sauce 55
Mushroom sauce 15
Mushroom sauce (Italian) 101
Mustard butter 89
Mustard sauce 16

Neapolitan tomato sauce 99
Newburg sauce 129
Nivernaise sauce 31
Normandy sauce 27
Nut custard 162

Onion purée sauce (Soubise sauce) 23
Onion sauce 16
Orange custard 162
Orange flower water sauce 171
Orange and lemon marinade 125
Orange sauce (Bigarade sauce) 45

Palois sauce 56
Panada 129
Paprika butter 90
Paprika sauce 30
Parmesan cheese dressing 152
Parsley sauce 17
Pepper sauce 42
Périgueux sauce 45
Pesto 103
Pickle barbecue sauce for beef 93
Piquant sauce 41
Piquant sauce, quick 145
Poivrade or pepper sauce 42
Portugaise sauce 136

Poulette sauce 30
Pouring sauce 9
Pouring sauce—roux method 11
Prawn butter 90
Prawn sauce 17
Princesse sauce 31

Quick sauces 141—5

Raisin sauce 130
Ravigote dressing 153
Ravigote sauce 27
Reform sauce 43
Rémoulade sauce 72
Robert sauce 41
Roux method 10—12
Rum butter (or rum hard sauce) 169
Rum sauce 166
Russian sauce 72

Sabayon sauce 179
Salad dressings 146—57
Salsa alla pizzaiola 99
Salsa verde (green dressing) 153
Sauce à la King 142
Sauce-boats 183
Sauce verte 69
Savoury butters 82—90
Shrimp butter 90
Shrimp sauce 17
Skordalia 67
Smitane or sour cream sauce 27
Smoked salmon butter 90
Soubise (or onion purée) sauce 23
Sour cream sauce 27
Soured cream dressing 154
Spiced white wine marinade 126
Stock for brown sauces 36
Suprême sauce 29
Swedish sauce 73
Sweet sauces 158—80

Sweet-sour sauce for fish 134
Sweet-sour sauce for pork 133
Sweet-sour sauce for
  vegetables 132
Syrup sauces 176

Tartare sauce 74
Tartare sauce (hot) 23
Thousand Island sauce 74
Tomato barbecue sauce 93
Tomato sauce, Neapolitan 99
Tomato sauces 135—8

Universal sauce 139

Vanilla sauce (blending
  method) 164
Vanilla sauce (roux method) 165

Velouté sauce 23—4
Victorian sauces 138—40
Vinaigrette dressing 150

Watercress sauce 75
Weinschaum sauce 178
Whisky butter (or whisky
  hard sauce) 170
White sauces:
  Classic white sauces
    18—31
  Simple savoury white sauces
    8—17
  Sweet white sauces 164—66
Wine marinade 126
Worcestershire sauce 139

Zabaglione sauce 177